# RECLAIMING SOUTHSIDE

## Praise for *Reclaiming Southside*

"In *Reclaiming Southside*, M. J. Coll recollects her life with its challenges and triumphs, starting when she was living in Southside, Richmond. She recalls living in other places, the women who meant a lot to her, and how she came back to Richmond, not really meaning to stay. Southside is south of the James River. At one time, Southside was a separate city—Manchester—and some of that separateness remains. M. J. has that personal feeling of separateness, a combination of many things including growing up working-class, having Latino heritage, and being a tomboy, an intellectual, and a lesbian. She has a lot to add to lesbian history through chronicling what being a lesbian has meant in her own life. Good reading and inspiring."

—Beth Marschak, founder of Richmond Lesbian-Feminist, lesbian and human rights activist, and coauthor of *Lesbian and Gay Richmond*

"*Reclaiming Southside* is a tender and heartfelt coming of age story that takes place through the fifties and sixties in the South, the burgeoning lesbian and feminist movements of the seventies in Iowa City, and the social changes of the eighties, nineties, and beyond. From her 'southern, Latino midwestern' perspective, Coll reminds us that life is big enough to hold family pain alongside familial beauty, rejection along with redemption, and big enough, ultimately, to bring us back to the people we always were."

—Elizabeth Ferris, editor of *Unspoken: Writers on Infertility, Miscarriage, and Stillbirth*

"In a tapestry woven from short, evocative scenes, Coll takes you on a journey that spans seven decades. Witness the transformation of a young girl's world as her idyllic summer mornings fishing with her father morph into a reality shadowed by violence. With humor and poignant honesty, she unveils moments of abuse, forgiveness, and the profound impact of powerful women.

"*Reclaiming Southside* is more than a coming-of-age story. It's a coming out story too. Coll explores tangled webs of sexuality, self-discovery, and the quiet strength found in facing one's truth. From encounters with the ethereal to a profound connection with animals, Coll's life unfolds in a kaleidoscope of experiences.

"Prepare to be captivated by a childhood forever marked by a father's duality and a mother's passive, but sometimes cruel, love; the resilience of the human spirit in the face of adversity; the solace found in unexpected connections, human and animal; and the power of humor to navigate the complexities of life.

"This is a story of resilience, self-acceptance, and the unwavering pursuit of a life reclaimed."

—Cindy Cunningham, founder of Wellspring Writing Collective and author of *Wild Woman: Memoir in Pieces*

## More Praise for *Reclaiming Southside*

"This book is a gift to our generation. While our paths may have been different, there are stories, thoughts, and feelings that LGBTQ people who grew up in the fifties and sixties will certainly recognize or identify with in this memoir. While reading this, I know people will say to themselves, 'Yes, that was me, too. I had forgotten, but that was me.'"

—Bill Harrison, cochair of the first Richmond Pride Festival in June 1979

"M. J. is a sensitive, black-eyed girl who escapes her wounded childhood in the capital of the Confederacy but returns to reclaim her home in later life. The charm of her memoir lies in its particulars: brewing Lucienne coffee in a tin pot, sitting cross-legged in the attic with a white candle and a Ouija board, and searching for fishing holes in Pocosham Creek with her grandmother. *Reclaiming Southside* is a heartfelt and heartwarming rite of passage."

—Douglas Jones, instructor at the Virginia Museum of Fine Arts

# RECLAIMING SOUTHSIDE

## M. J. COLL

Brandylane Publishers, Inc.
*Publishing books since 1985*

Copyright © 2024 by M. J. Coll

All rights reserved. No part of this book may be reproduced in any form or by any electronic or mechanical means, or the facilitation thereof, including information storage and retrieval systems, without permission in writing from the publisher, except in the case of brief quotations published in articles and reviews. Any educational institution wishing to photocopy part or all of the work for classroom use, or individual researchers who would like to obtain permission to reprint the work for educational purposes, should contact the publisher.

ISBN: 978-1-962416-47-4
Library of Congress Control Number: 2024910935

*Designed by Sami Langston*
*Project managed by Ceci Hughes*

Printed in the United States of America

Published by
Brandylane Publishers, Inc.
5 S. 1st Street
Richmond, Virginia 23219

brandylanepublishers.com

*This book is dedicated to all the wonderful leaders of the women's and LGBTQ communities. Without their vision and persistence, it would be a very different world.*

# Contents

Introduction ........................................................................................... 1
Part One: Childhood ............................................................................ 5
    Comfort Food ................................................................................ 7
    Grandmother's House in the Mountains ..................................... 8
    Grandmother Mary ..................................................................... 10
    Grandfather Will ......................................................................... 12
    Chanel No. 5 ................................................................................ 13
    Answers ........................................................................................ 15
    Divorce ......................................................................................... 17
    Champ .......................................................................................... 19
    Misha and Pit .............................................................................. 21
    Ponies ........................................................................................... 23
    The Basement .............................................................................. 25
    The Contest ................................................................................. 26
    Attic Adventures ......................................................................... 27
    Charm School .............................................................................. 29
    My Portrait .................................................................................. 30
    Baptism ........................................................................................ 31
    Hurricane ..................................................................................... 32
    Reoccurring Dream .................................................................... 33
    Rage Reaction .............................................................................. 34
    Summer Vacation ........................................................................ 36
    Pier Fishing ................................................................................. 38
    A Heaping Helping of Fear and Guilt ...................................... 39
    Cherish ......................................................................................... 41
    Goodbye ....................................................................................... 43
    The Day of the Dead .................................................................. 44
    Coffee and Magnolias ................................................................. 45
    Then and Now ............................................................................. 46
Part Two: College and Coming Out .................................................. 47
    Freedom ....................................................................................... 49
    Protests ........................................................................................ 51
    Iowa City ..................................................................................... 53
    Coming Out ................................................................................ 55
    Mom ............................................................................................. 58
    Haunted in Solon ........................................................................ 59
    Tiffin ............................................................................................. 62
    Monica ......................................................................................... 63
    The Longest Winter .................................................................... 65

**Part Three: Coming Home** ............................................................. **67**
    Healing ............................................................................................ 69
    Jennifer ........................................................................................... 72
    Summer Festivals ......................................................................... 74
    Things Unsaid ............................................................................... 76
    Alzheimer's .................................................................................... 77
    Drinking ......................................................................................... 79
    Secrets ............................................................................................ 80
    End of Summer ............................................................................ 81
**Part Four: Adulthood** ..................................................................... **83**
    Ten Sounds of Summer ............................................................. 85
    Living in the Family Home ...................................................... 86
    Marriage Equality ........................................................................ 88
    Graduate School .......................................................................... 90
    Teaching ......................................................................................... 92
    One Thing I Learned .................................................................. 93
    Therapy .......................................................................................... 94
    Stressful Dreams ......................................................................... 96
    The Apology ................................................................................. 98
    Where They Are Now .............................................................. 100
    Gay in RVA ................................................................................. 101
**About the Author** .......................................................................... **103**

# Introduction

When I was little, and before my dad became violent, he and I would spend most summer mornings by Pocosham Creek, fishing for blue gills. We both had special poles that we also used for fishing at the Outer Banks. Ancient trees lined the small creek, and we sat cradled in their roots. I was never as happy as when I went fishing with my dad. He would be uncommonly relaxed and tell awful puns and dad jokes.

"Knock, knock," he would start, grinning.
"Who's there?" I'd respond eagerly.
"Orange."
"Orange who?"
"Orange you glad you opened the door?"

I loved our times together, and I adored him. I wanted to be like his son. I dressed like him and walked like him—whenever he wore brown pants and black collared shirts, so did I.

I grew up in Southside before the annexation in 1970. Our small farmhouse was still in Chesterfield, and groceries and milk were delivered to our back porch. Our road was a narrow, two-lane road that teenagers often drag raced down, and sometimes they missed the sudden turn before the concrete bridge over the creek, ending up in our front field. Broad Rock Road was a small street with one store on the corner of Walmsley Boulevard that sold a little bit of everything, including a large assortment of penny candy for kids. Brookbury was still a working farm where cows grazed in open fields. My best friend Pam and I would often ride our horses through the woods there to pick blackberries in the pastures. We would carry mounds of berries home in large Lucienne coffee tins, which swam with the lovely purple berry juice.

One of my favorite memories of Pam, who lived down the road in a big ranch house with three older brothers, was when we went trick-or-treating one year. We were eight and ten years old and dressed as witches with black hats and brooms. We felt free from parental control and full of joy as we ran through dozens of front yards, giggling and yelling "trick or treat!" as we rang the doorbells. Everyone who gave us treats commented on how glad they were to see us. At the end of the night, we split the candy fifty-fifty.

In the fall, the neighborhood kids would play tag football in their backyards. I was athletic, but sometimes these games got rough for me because most of the players were older, and boys. Often, I opted to ride my blue bicycle instead, bouncing along the neighborhood's gravel roads. Sometimes we rode together as a group, flying down the quiet back roads in a cluster of blue and red bicycles.

In the winter, Pam and I used the steep incline beyond the concrete bridge for sledding. My sled had iron runners and a wooden platform to lie on. One afternoon, my dad towed a whole line of our sleds up the hill behind his heavy green Chrysler. It was so exciting to slip and slide up the steep hill. I spent most winter days playing in the deep snow, building snowmen and forts. It was cold, but I didn't feel it. When I came home, my mom would put my wet mittens and socks on the radiators to dry them out. Then, she would fix homemade hot chocolate, and we would watch *I Love Lucy* reruns on our black-and-white TV while sitting together on our comfortable green couch.

In the spring, all of the yards in the neighborhood would be full of jonquils and blooming dogwood trees. On Easter, Dad, who was famous for his corny sense of humor, would hide Easter eggs in creative new places, like in tree limbs, on car tires, and behind a row of spring flowers in our yard. In early April, just as the weather began to warm up, our family would drive to Kitty Hawk, North Carolina, to go pier fishing. Dad would often brag about his great fishing skills, but I have many photos of my mother holding a rod with a mullet on the end of the line.

Several of the kids I grew up with have returned to Southside as adults, including me. These days, I live in the same house where my mom dried my socks and mittens on the radiators by the windows. My parents are gone now, and the neighborhood and I have both changed. When it is cold outside, I hang out by the fireplace and read a good book. I still love Pocosham Creek, and every summer I watch fireflies dance in my front yard as the sun goes down.

*Introduction*

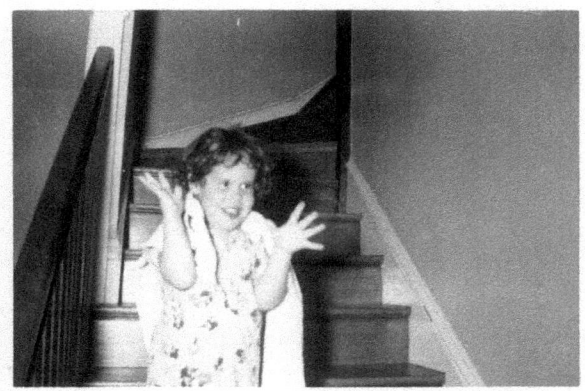

# Part One:

# *Childhood*

(1950s and 1960s, five to eighteen years old)

# Comfort Food

Throughout my childhood, I remember eating arroz con pollo on Sunday afternoons after church. My mother, Elaine, learned to cook Puerto Rican recipes from my father's mother, who only spoke Spanish and still lived in Luquillo, where my dad, John, grew up. The chicken was tender, and the yellow saffron rice was soft but not mushy. For dessert, my mother would make flan. The sweetness was intoxicating. We drank sweet tea, which was very southern. Lots of sugar hid the tang of the tea.

We had lunch in the middle of the day after church, and we always ate together, a practice that has fallen out of fashion today. My mother had a love-hate relationship with food, just as I do today. She and I both loved sugary treats like ice cream, which we binged and then avoided. The foods she loved, like fried chicken, mashed potatoes, and apple pie, were loaded with calories, and her weight fluctuated up and down, as mine does today. She joined Weight Watchers to help with these fluctuations and constantly recorded her calories on cards that she kept in metal index card boxes. She had a very strict idea of the importance of being thin and spent her life trying to achieve that goal. I still have several of those boxes filled with cards with the foods she ate and her calorie totals for the day.

I find now that my comfort foods are often something crunchy, like pretzels or those blue corn chips you can buy in a jumbo bag—very different foods from what my mother and I would eat together. But the southern part of me swoons at the sight and smell of fried chicken and mashed potatoes.

# Grandmother's House in the Mountains

The mint green Chrysler my parents owned in the fifties was built like a tank. The back seat, where I stretched out to sleep on longer trips, held me like a nice, soft featherbed. The trips from Richmond to the Valley to see Grandmother Mary felt like trips across country—from a large city to a tiny town in the middle of the countryside. Churchville had a population of about two hundred back then. There were two churches, one gas station, and a café.

My grandparents lived outside of Churchville on a long dirt road. My grandmother's people were from the area, and driving by houses, I would see our family's name on several mailboxes. My grandfather came from one of the adjacent counties. Their house was small and squat, with chickens outside. My grandfather, Will, had built the house with his own hands. There was electricity, but no bathrooms except for an outhouse out back next to a big barn. The smell from both places was strong. I didn't like using the outhouse, particularly not at night when bears were out, wandering the countryside.

The front porch overlooked the trees of the Blue Ridge Mountains, and a path led down to the river where we parked our car and walked across a hanging bridge. Panda, the black-and-tan dog that my grandmother loved, always met us at the end of the bridge and walked with us up to the house. The front porch had a hanging swing with a rope for the kids to swing by themselves. There was a painting in the hallway of beautiful spotted hunting dogs: springer spaniels with flowing tails and noses pointed toward the game they were stalking. I loved all of it.

My grandmother loved to tell stories about black bears that would wander up to the house and look in the windows on the porch. She told us how she would go upstairs and fire a shotgun out of the window to scare them away. She described the "thump, thump, thump" as they would run off the wooden porch. "A bear might get you," my dad liked to tell me when I asked to visit the outhouse in the dark. I believed him and stayed on my comfortable couch.

When all twenty of my aunts and uncles and cousins got together for Thanksgiving, it was quite a sight. It was heavenly for an only child like me, who was often lonely. There were lots of kinfolk to play with in the front yard and talk to on the porch. An abundance of food would be piled on the kitchen table, brought by the women relatives—country food—fried chicken, mashed potatoes, and pies of all sorts. These gatherings brought out the best in us—love and comfort—and I miss these times so much.

# Grandmother Mary

It feels as though I have always lived in my parents' old farmhouse in Southside. This is the place I call home. I'm particularly connected to the little house out back where my grandmother lived when I was nine and she was seventy-nine, just after her much-loved husband had died. It was (and still is) a small, two-room wooden house. There was an old tin roof where the rain lulled her to sleep; a woodstove for heat; and sliding windows that let in the cool night air. She would sleep on a cot in front of the sliding windows, and she would make her cup of coffee every morning on that woodstove: Lucienne coffee from a tin. I was named after her, and she always called me her "black-eyed child." She told me she could see "rocks sparkling on the hill" at night through the windows, and I wanted to go with her to look for those precious stones that sparkled on that hill at night.

Mary was a fisherman like me, and she and I spent hours walking Pocosham Creek, chattering away and looking for fishing holes. She was in her early eighties then, but had the energy of someone much younger, and I had trouble keeping up with her on my short little legs. She was not tall, but she was quick. During one of our conversations together, I told her, "I am taller than you." She just looked at me with those beady brown eyes and said, "No you aren't." I said, "I am taller than Inky," who was our small black dog. She looked at me over her glasses and said, "Maybe." She was not one of those grandmothers who let their grandchildren get away with anything.

She and my grandfather had five children and had lived in the Shenandoah Valley, which at the time was deep country. I am sure it was a hard life for them since it was a small farming community. My grandfather was a teacher and a farmer, and my grandmother was a farmer and a homemaker.

Grandmother Mary and my mother had an oil-and-water kind of relationship. Mom was a "pearls and fur coat" gal, and Grandmother Mary was a "dirty shoes and hiking in the mountains" gal. I don't think they agreed on much. My grandmother's favorite saying was "hitch your wagon to a star," and my mother's favorite comment was "I've seen better." This tug-of-war constantly simmered under the surface. Shortly after Grandmother Mary came to live with us, it erupted outside on the front porch. My grandmother said, "You are spoiling her." And my mother countered with, "No, I'm not." When they noticed that I was standing right there listening, they both changed the subject. Who should I have trusted?

My grandmother had been living in the room that later would become my dad's room, but after that fight, she moved to the little house out back, which had been an office when the house was built in 1938. After a year or two, she told us she was going to live with Uncle Clyde at his farm, near her old house. I was devastated. How could she leave me?

# Grandfather Will

Grandfather Will was in his early eighties when I met him. He was older than Grandmother Mary, who was in her late seventies during most of my memories of her. He had been a handsome, German-looking fellow (his ancestors had come from Germany in the eighteen hundreds), with black hair and a handlebar mustache. He had been a history teacher and had met my grandmother at a Churchville baseball game in his early twenties. It was love at first sight, and he moved to the area to be with her. It must have taken him forever to build the family home by hand since it was way out in the country, and everything had to be hauled in by truck and then carried over the swinging bridge across the river. The two-level, wooden house had a wraparound porch in the front, which was traditional for mountain houses in the Shenandoah Valley at the turn of the century. It was outside of the town but not far enough to be isolated.

My grandfather loved my grandmother and was always complimenting her cooking. The one thing he did not have going for him was his missing eye. He had lost it on a barbed wire fence while being chased by yellow jackets before I was born. He didn't always wear an eye patch, and often, his exposed eye socket was in plain sight. It hurt to look at that empty socket and to imagine the barbs that had been lodged in his eye—painful to think about.

At the end of his life, my grandfather lived in a nursing home outside of Waynesboro. We visited him a few Sundays each year, and each time, he would be lying on the bed, staring at the ceiling. The nurses would tell us about how he would wander and be found walking down the road toward the old farmhouse. He wanted to go home.

Soon after my grandfather died, my Uncle Clyde, who lived closest to the family home, sold it. He didn't think he could keep it up well. The house is still there at the end of the gravel road, across the river. I dream of it often, and all the love that was for me there.

# Chanel No. 5

Whenever I smell the tangy but sweet scent of Chanel No. 5, I think of my mother. She never left the house without a splash of it behind her ear. In the fifties and sixties, Chanel No. 5 was the most popular perfume to wear—even Marilyn Monroe famously said that all she wore to bed was Chanel No. 5.

My mother was a very proper lady—always staying inside the boundaries of convention. As a doctor's wife she felt she had certain rules to follow, and she followed them faithfully. The rules, as I understood them, were to always be well-dressed in public, to not raise your voice, and to keep family business at home. In addition to those three, the most important rule was to not speak your mind. "Whatever comes up, comes out" was to be avoided.

My mother and I shopped at the downtown Miller & Rhoads and Thalhimers stores in downtown Richmond on Fridays, which were see-and-be-seen events. We would eat at the upstairs restaurant, not the downstairs cafeteria, because all the well-dressed ladies and their well-dressed children ate at the upstairs restaurant. Downstairs was too cheap for us. To be a well-dressed girl meant to wear dresses, stockings, and Mary Jane patent leather shoes. I hated the tightness of the shoes and dresses and how confined I felt. I hated those shopping sprees. One Friday, I created a scene by crying and wailing to go home. We were downstairs by the elevator, in the middle of the crowd of women and children. My mother refused, yelling at me and jerking my hand. This push-pull conflict between us was evident all our lives. I wanted one thing, and she wanted something totally different.

We were constantly divided between what each of us wanted. On the one side of this divide was me—short, brown-haired, wearing brown pants, tennis shoes, and a ratty T-shirt, arms crossed, crying out, "I just want to ride horses, shoot guns, join the Boy Scouts, and play baseball." On the other side of the divide was my mother—a woman over forty with dyed brown hair, wearing blue cat-eye glasses, high heels, and a fur wrap around her shoulders saying, "M. J., young ladies do not swim without their shirts. They do not climb trees or ride bicycles." It was a stand-off where she had the upper hand. She usually ended the fight by saying, "I will tell your father about this." Even though my dad was my fishing and backyard-repair friend, he deferred to my mother's ideas of who I should become. He had always wanted a son, and I was as close as he would get to his dream because of my tomboy habits, but these masculine tendencies were always a disappointment to her, and therefore to him.

On my dresser at home now is her half-empty bottle of Channel No. 5. The bittersweet smell brings back memories of her.

14

# Answers

My father was a very good-looking guy, and my mom and I always felt kind of special to be in his company in public. I remember how he looked and sounded when he smiled-his dark eyes crinkling and that great laugh he had. People flocked to him, the way they do to a movie star. When I was young, he was the earth, and I was the moon that revolved around him. The problem was he felt that way about himself too. He never left the house without combing his black hair just right and dressing in an expensive suit and tie. His aftershave still haunts me—Old Spice, which smelled of the salty sea. He wore his hats with the brim turned to the side in a jaunty way, saying, "Pay attention. I am here."

In his friends and relatives' eyes, my father could do no wrong. As a well-educated doctor who was Hollywood-handsome, he could get away with murder. Anything he said had to be true to the people he dealt with daily. It reminds me of the well-known joke: What is the difference between God and a doctor? At least God knows he is not a doctor.

It took me a long time to figure out his personality, and it took even longer for me to realize the danger of disagreeing with him. His ego was very fragile, and it seemed he felt everything was about him.

I was his fishing buddy, and we spent hours fishing for blue gills at Pocosham Creek or mullet and channel bass on the pier at Nags Head. I loved fishing with him—except for the part where we had to leave the fish on the pier to flop helplessly. I was eight years old when I realized the fish were flopping to get back to the water and save themselves, and when I finally understood this, I panicked at the sight. My father told me that fish don't feel pain like humans do, but I didn't believe him or want to do this horrible activity anymore. I would have liked to have thrown them back, but I knew Daddy would be mad at losing his catch. I started putting them out of their misery by hitting them on the head with a knife handle. In my mind, a quick death was better than a slow one. Daddy didn't like this. The fish wouldn't be as fresh to eat. At the age of eight, I stopped fishing with him, and he liked that even less.

This was the beginning of the unraveling of our relationship. I think my father took my changing my mind about fishing very personally. For a long time, I hoped he could be more objective, but he was one of those people who thought everything was about him. He saw my lack of interest in fishing with him as rejection, and he hated being told no. In retrospect, I am not sure I could have acted any differently. The sight of anything or anyone suffering is painful to me. I always feel other people's feelings and try extremely hard to be kind and not cause harm to any living beings, which of course included my dad. I could have expressed this to him directly if our family wasn't so oriented toward secrets. I do regret not talking about it while he was alive.

By the time my teenage years rolled around, our disagreements were much more serious, and sometimes I feared for my life. During one of our screaming fights, one of my friends, Robert, happened to call on the phone. Robert heard the screaming on the other end of the phone, called the police, and raced over in his car to save me. The fight was over by the time he got to the house, and the police never came or called to check in. Perhaps their tolerance was because my dad was a doctor. Domestic violence was not taken very seriously during the sixties, and a man's home was his castle, as my mom constantly reminded me. My mother would say, "It's a man's world, M. J." I would reply, "But what about us? We live in this world too." She would shrug.

I still wonder if my dad had an undiagnosed personality disorder. He may have been an alcoholic as well. I'll never know the answers to these questions until he and I meet again in the next world, heaven. I will have lots of questions for him then.

# Divorce

I remember standing at the top of the stairs, listening to them yell at each other in the living room. I was a preteen, full of emotion, and they were fighting over who would get the house when they divorced. Not *if* they divorced, but *when*. I was frozen with fear. Mom's tone was sharp; she was furious. "It is mine. I deserve it," she barked at Dad.

"Okay, whatever you want," was his response in the calm voice that he often had before exploding in anger.

This was a reversal of their usual roles, in which Mom usually gave in and said, "Whatever you want, John."

I had no idea they were having problems. I was just a kid finding out I lived in a house full of secrets. I didn't know what to do. In hindsight, my dad's solo fishing trips with no fish to show for the effort were probably a sign. I had heard my mom speak of other women in conversations between her and my father. Then there was his whispering on the phone behind closed doors. Who was he talking to? Why was it a secret?

When I was an adult in my thirties, the certified nursing assistants we hired to care for my mother complained to me about my father's unwanted sexual advances. My dad wasn't doing much to help with my mom's care, and he was seriously flirting with the CNAs. He even told one of them that sex with him would only take a few minutes, so what was the big deal? They wanted me to protect them from him. It made me realize my mother had probably been right all along.

Standing on the stairs that night as a young girl, I felt my heart racing. Neither my mother nor my father was a particularly good parent, but together, they canceled each other out and kept each other from doing a lot of harm to me. I knew the courts would probably award custody to my mother because that was typical at that time. Her Bible-thumping, Evangelical ways drove me crazy. I knew I couldn't live with her, but I was afraid of him. After I stopped fishing with dad, he became volatile. His temper was frightening and uncontrolled. Yelling. Screaming. Hitting me. Hitting the dog. Had he always been this way? I was not sure if he had behaved like this when I was a small child too, but it certainly was true now. There were no good choices for me.

My anxiety pushed me forward, like electricity running down my body, head to toe. I jumped down the stairs in tears and threw myself into the middle of their drama.

"Please don't break up," I sobbed.

They stopped fighting, silent and shocked.

Standing before them, crying very real tears, I must have looked pitiful. In hindsight, I have deep regrets. Would we have all been happier if I had not intervened and they could have had separate lives?

# Champ

My four-legged friends were my best friends growing up. I couldn't count on humans to love me, but dogs, cats, and horses were always there to support me. We got Champ as a small black beagle after my mother's dogs, Inky and Fluff, died. Champ had a white diamond on her chest and floppy black ears that waved behind her as she ran.

I remember Inky and Fluff's deaths but not their lives since I had been so young when they passed. Inky's heart attack in our basement and Fluff's mysterious beating were my first tastes of death and loss. I was under six years old when we found Fluff beaten to death in our top field, blood running from her beautiful ears, and we never found out who killed her. Because we lived on a farm, my parents saw animals as just animals. Even though my mother had a soft spot for indoor animals, they were not her friends, which is how I have always viewed animals.

Champ and I grew up together. When got her as a puppy, I was allowed to choose her name. I was already a sports buff at seven, so I came up with the name "Champ" for champion. She seemed to know I picked her out and named her because almost from day one, she trailed me like a little shadow. Wherever I went, Champ went too. She and I would spend all day together roaming the fields and the forest beside our property until it was dusk, and Mom called me inside with her ship's bell. Champ and I would sit side by side together in the top field where the horses pastured, and I would dream of a future filled with basketball, softball, and being a boy scout. I think she dreamt of a future filled with following me around. I have lots of old photos of Mom and Champ in the backyard. One of my favorites is of Mom on her plastic and nylon folding chair and Champ sniffing something on the ground nearby.

Soon after we got Champ, we added a collie named Star and several ponies to our menagerie. The most memorable pony was a gray pinto stallion named Dixie, who had white markings on his left side that looked like North and South America. I rode Dixie western style all over the property, up and down the hills, and along the creek. He was always glad to see me and never bucked me off on our rides.

Star was a sweet collie, whose brown eyes twinkled and tail wagged when she saw me. But she had a wandering nature. She always wandered up the gravel road to visit the neighbors in the Quonset hut who fed her. Maybe they fed her better food than we did, or maybe it was a quieter household with no yelling, but when I was a teenager, Star left us and moved in with them. By then, she and Champ were old dogs, and they had been friends for ten years or more, so Champ began to visit Star at the Quonset hut house. When I went away to college in Iowa, Champ must have felt left behind and lonely, and she started to visit Star more regularly. During my first year at college, Champ was struck by a car while crossing our road to see Star. She died before I got to say goodbye to her.

# Misha and Pit

Misha was a Siamese cat that my mother acquired when I was young. Misha had a very loud voice and let you know what she thought about everything. Misha would sit with my mother on the couch while she watched TV, and my mother would run her hands along Misha's black and silver coat. Then she was relegated to the basement and seldom went outside. I never understood why my mother made this decision—she had always been a little paranoid and suspicious, and maybe she thought Misha could pass something to us. Misha would sleep on the top steps of the basement, so my mother put a sign on the basement door that said, "Beware of cat on the stairs," so she would not trip over Misha on her way to do laundry downstairs.

In my late teens, when I was going for one of my Sunday drives as I learned to drive, I found a black and brown kitten running down a side street in a neighborhood. I brought her home and named her Pit for "bottomless pit" since she never stopped eating—probably because she had been a stray as a baby. She and Misha became inseparable, and they lived in the basement together. When you saw one cat, you saw the other—on the flagstone or relaxing on the back porch steps. I learned from Misha and Pit, and Champ and Star, that the bonds between animals are just as strong as those between humans.

When Misha became older and more fragile, she had an accident on the back porch. She jumped off the back porch and landed on the flagstone walkway extremely hard. She broke her jaw. The vet suggested that she would not heal well from such a devastating injury, so my parents had her put to sleep. Her best friend, Pit, watched for her to come home for several days. She ran to the door when we went inside. My parents started keeping her in the basement full-time because she was so obviously upset. I would hang out in the basement, too, petting and soothing her by talking to her. Pit would run from room to room in the basement, meowing. A few days after Misha died, Pit had a heart attack, dying from a broken heart.

# Ponies

We had a small herd of ponies on the farm when I was growing up—in addition to Dixie, the sweet stallion who had a white imprint of North and South America on his left side, we also had Gypsy, a brown mare, who gave birth to Bonita (which is Spanish for "pretty"), and later Major, the beautiful palomino gelding who was supposed to be my riding pony when I outgrew the others. My best friend Pam also had horses, and she and I rode our horses and ponies every weekend.

I also rode horses at the small private school I attended. The school was down the country road a few minutes from my house and had a lake for swimming in the summer and a ring to ride horses in shows for family and friends. I couldn't bring Dixie to these shows because he was a stallion and might start a fight with one of the geldings.

We bought Major when I was in high school, after Dixie had been traded to a nearby farm. He was beautiful but very wild. He had light blue eyes, a yellow coat, and a white mane. It took me a while to figure out his true nature because he was so pretty. My first indication of his personality was when he tried to rip my legs on the barbed-wire fence leading to the top field. I told myself he didn't mean to hurt me, but I was wrong. One day while riding in the top field, he started to spin like a top. It was too much for me. I tried to rein him in and put him under control, but he got mad and spun faster. I flew off the saddle like a missile, landing extremely hard. I lay there for a long time, unable to get up. My back was badly hurt, and I thought I might pass out. As I lay there, I saw Major twirling and spinning his way toward the barn, and I understood that he had meant to throw me off. I silently sobbed, crawled painfully to the fence, opened the gate, and dragged myself up to the house. Luckily, I had not broken any bones. The common advice at the time was to always get back on the horse after you had been thrown off, but I could not get back on. I had been too hurt. I never rode Major again and he was rehomed. I stopped riding altogether after being hurt in this way. The other ponies became more like lawn ornaments and pets.

# The Basement

I think all children harbor some fear of basements. There is something about the dank darkness that elicits fear and anxiety of "things that go bump in the night." But for me, even as an adult, I *know* something is down there looking out for me.

Our house was built in 1938, and the basement windows open inward so that a truck could dump coal into the storage units in the basement that fueled the furnace. The coal-burning furnace has long been replaced, and the chimney in the middle of the room is no longer used. A bathroom and shower were put in down there in the forties, at the back of the basement wall. My family bought the house in the early fifties from the original family. My father got a loan from my grandfather for a thousand dollars to buy the house and property, which must have seemed like a lot of money at the time.

In the basement, I have a strong sense of eyes following me. Friends have even told me they experience the same thing in my basement. Eyes seem to follow you from the side room, which is off from the furnace. As a child, I would run up the basement stairs to get away from that feeling of being watched. Perhaps those eyes were my dad, who always wanted to be in the basement with me, or my mom, who made sure we got upstairs right away when we had to go down there.

Growing up, I often found arrowheads in our yard, as well as Civil War bullets in the top field, and I know that there is history in the area that predates our little brick farmhouse. But unlike the foreboding spirit in the basement, my sense is that a guardian watches over the house itself. I feel protected here, as if there is a guardian angel. As an outsider in my own family, I was more in tune with other energies in the area, and I needed to feel like someone was watching over me, protecting me. Real or imaginary, I felt I had a protector when I was growing up.

# The Contest

While my mother would do laundry in the basement, I would sit on my knees on the floor, coloring in a coloring book and playing with marbles. The floor was cold gray concrete and chilled my skin through my pants, but it was level and great for shooting marbles. I had all kinds of colored marbles and was very proud of my collection. I was also proud of my ability to color well. My father was a painter and photographer, as well as a doctor, and I inherited his eye for framing a shot with a camera, and for capturing the emotion in a scene with broad strokes of oil paint.

Pam was the only other girl in the neighborhood, and she lived down the road from my house. Pam had three brothers, and her parents would let all four of them run wild. If I wanted company my own age, Pam was my only choice. She was a year older than me and in a different grade in school, but she and I both loved archery and riding our horses bareback across the open fields. Our age difference contributed to competitions, which sprang up between us. Everything was fair game for competition, like who could pick the most berries, on foot or on horseback.

One morning, she and I were on the basement floor while mom was sorting the laundry. We were in a contest to see who could color a picture best. Pam told me that my mother had been choosing me even though I wasn't as good as she was. "No way," I said. Pam suggested we color pictures to prove her point; I would color messily, outside the lines and with funny colors, while she would color neatly. Once our masterpieces were completed, and Pam's was nicely colored inside the lines, we called my mom to "choose the best one." Mom quickly chose my picture, and after she left the room, Pam laughed and said, "I told you so." I felt shocked and a bit scared because this was not the outcome I had expected. I had thought my mother would be a fair judge of our work, and I began to question whether anyone was truly fair and impartial.

# Attic Adventures

Pam's father was an engineer who drove a red-hot sports car and was seldom home. Her mother was an artist who dealt with the chaos at home by focusing on her painting. One afternoon, as I walked out Pam's front door to go home, my blue bicycle crashed down to the ground right in front of me. Her brothers had hoisted the bike to the top of a high tree and waited for me to come outside to drop it. They laughed and laughed. Those boys were a tough crowd. Pam was basically on her own, a free agent. Meanwhile, my mom worried about me and watched my every move, and I hated it.

"M. J., you need to be home by five o'clock."

"M. J., don't ride your bike to the Tyler's house."

"M. J., I wish you wouldn't spend so much time at Pam's house."

I hated the nagging. I felt trapped by her rules, so Pam and I spent hours hidden away from her sight in the attic above the garage. We would make each other laugh by jumping out the back window of the attic. The fall from this window was at least ten feet—exhilarating and terrifying at the same time. Bright yellow forsythias were planted below the window, and we bounced when we hit the shrubs. Since we were sixty pounds apiece, the challenge was to launch ourselves out of the window, free fall for several feet, and land on the bushes, seeing how many times we could bounce before hitting the ground—hopefully not so hard that we broke bones.

Other times, we would spend whole afternoons by the light of the back window, throwing dice and capturing or losing Park Place in Monopoly.

Once, we found a Ouija Board at Pam's house. The garage was packed with junk and the board was sitting in a corner by itself—almost like it was asking to be found. We knew that you could use the board to talk to dead people. *What fun! What do dead people have to say to us? Are we going to be rich when we grow up?*

The problem was we didn't know any dead people to talk to. Both of our sets of grandparents were very much alive. I mentioned the name of someone I heard had died recently on the six o'clock news, which my parents watched every night: Bishop Pike. I only knew his name and did not know anything about his story. To be honest, I'll bet I didn't know what a bishop was, either. We decided to get in touch with him anyway.

Laughing all the way, we climbed the garage door and wiggled through the entrance to the attic, Ouija Board and white candle clutched in our dirty little hands. We sat crossed-legged, the Ouija Board on our knees. We lit the candle, and I used a bit of candle wax to prop it up beside us on the floorboards. Then we closed our eyes for a moment to ask for the spirit of Bishop Pike to appear.

On the front of the board, "yes" and "no" were printed on opposite sides. Printed between these words were the letters of the alphabet. The letters were ornate, like they belonged in the eighteen hundreds rather than the nineteen fifties. I put the small plastic triangle in the middle of the board; Pam and I both put our hands on it, and a zap of electricity ran through our fingers.

Our two pairs of eyes watched the pointer like hawks. Nothing was going to slip past us.

Minutes passed. We stared at the pointer, willing it to move. The sun shone on the back window. Birds chirped. I could hear Champ barking at a squirrel. Life went on as usual.

"Hello? Is anybody there?"

Then the pointer began to move slowly on the board.

"Cut that out."

"I'm not doing anything."

"Very funny."

"No . . . really."

The plastic pointer continued to move as if it had a mind of its own. Slowly, with jerky movements, it drifted to the "yes" section of the board.

"Do you have anything you want to tell us?" I asked quietly.

The pointer stopped moving. We heard a loud sound, like someone knocking on a wooden door. A cold wind came through the attic, blowing out our half-burned candle and submerging us in darkness. We both screamed and ran for the entrance, scrambling out of the garage and into the welcome sunlight.

After that day, I put the Ouija Board at the back of my closet, and it stayed there for as long as I can remember.

# Charm School

As a tomboy and soon-to-be lesbian feminist, it felt as though there was no place for me growing up in Richmond. There were no role models for me on TV or in real life, though my maiden aunt Ida, whom everyone felt sorry for, may have been an early feminist. Growing up, I rode horses and fired guns. I played sports and was very good at baseball and basketball. I wanted to be a boy scout because they got to camp out and do all my favorite things. But my only options for sanctioned extracurriculars were cotillion, charm school, tutus, and dance class.

The charm school teacher must have understood who I was because when we had to walk down the runway, balancing a book on our heads to show how graceful we were, she let me wear riding pants and carry a riding crop. I am sure that was a sight. I never got out of piano lessons, but after much crying and pleading, I became a proud charm school dropout.

Unlike my charm school teacher, Miss F., my tap dance teacher, did not cut me any slack. She made us all pose for the cameras at our dance recitals at the Mosque Theater every fall and spring. I still have a photo of myself in a red, white, and blue dance outfit, carrying a baton, smiling (falsely) for the camera.

Growing up, the acronym LGBTQ didn't exist. "Queer" was the closest word for describing my identity, but if some kid called me a queer on the playground, I fought them over it. I didn't even know what the word meant; I just knew it was a really bad thing. I am happy that people now have more options than I had growing up and that they don't have to go through the trials of charm school and dance classes if they don't really want to do those things.

# My Portrait

I kept it stored away in the basement. It was not a portrait of me as I really was; rather, it was a vision of who my parents wanted me to become. At nine years old, I was a rough and tumble tomboy who had short, curly hair, wore pants, rode horses, and shot guns. But the girl in the portrait looked like a teenager, with long dark hair that fell in waves across her face. Her brown eyes looked directly at the artist with an honest, straightforward gaze. Her eyebrows swept across the top of her face and her lips were full and red; she was probably wearing lipstick. She was thin, and a soft blue blouse sat gracefully on her shoulders. It was a fantasy.

It was a large portrait, with a lovely, ornate, light wood frame. It obviously had taken some time to draw and frame. I hadn't sat for it as I did for the portrait Pam's mother did when I was eight. That portrait showed a smiling kid, short-haired with a brown button-down shirt, and captured the real M. J. at the time, full of life and love for adventure. That kid was not a lady of intrigue.

That portrait hung over the piano in the living room, to the right of the large black-and-white TV, for many years. The other portrait, the one of the red-lipped young lady, hung in our den for a long time. I always felt like it was somehow accusing me of something—maybe of falling short of expectations, of not being the lady I was I was born to be. After I moved back home as I adult, I stored this portrait in the basement. Like the portrait of Dorian Gray, it haunted me—until I dropped it off at a Quaker thrift store bin.

# Baptism

I went to an old Southern Baptist church down the street from my house. My mother was a Methodist and my father a Catholic, and this church was the local compromise. I would walk to church on Sunday mornings and sit in the back on a wooden pew, fascinated by our pastor. He was a tall, silver-haired man with a booming voice. The subject of his lessons was often hellfire, damnation, and sin. There were lots of sermons on sin. It seemed that most of the things I wanted to do as a kid were sinful to these people. Playing cards and dancing were two of the top sins.

I wanted to be a good kid. I wanted my mother, who often quoted the Bible, to love me. So, I chose to be baptized in the church. Honestly, I didn't really choose; rather, I went along with what was asked from the pulpit—with special music—of everyone in the church: to go to the front every week and to say, "yes, I will be saved." My mom was pleased with my choice.

In the front of the church behind the wooden pulpit, sat a beautiful stained glass window of St. John the Baptist in the river, baptizing Jesus. The Holy Spirit was flying down from heaven to testify to his approval. There was a baptismal pool up front as well. On the day of my baptism, my mother dressed in her church hat, fancy dress, and fur coat and sat in the first row. I came out from the side of the altar in a thin white coverall. I was a teenager at the time, but still small, barely five feet tall. The minister waited for me in the pool in his black suit. He smiled and moved me forward. I climbed into the water and searched for the rock they had on the bottom for the little kids to stand on. I found it and stood up straight. He leaned me over backward, and as he immersed me in the water, the rock came out from under me, and I tumbled backward into the pool. As I sank down to the bottom of the cool water, I thought, *Am I going to be reborn and die on the same day?* I climbed out of the pool, shaking myself off like a wet dog. I could hear my mother laughing loudly from the front row. She had a very distinct, high-pitched laugh.

# Hurricane

I glance sideways at the
living room television as
the wooden pier collapses,
plank by plank.

You have me by the throat.
Big hands tighten
behind black eyes.
An ocean churns.

My mother is by my side,
small and still, a lifeboat
bobbing in dangerous
seas.

# Reoccurring Dream

She was afraid of the dark—a little girl who heard monsters under her bed and in her closet. They were so loud, these monsters, that her mother put a bed in her room so she could sleep there, part of the night, for her daughter's sake. When the sun went down, the front yard that was so friendly and welcoming by day became a place filled with large animals and terror. The black bear who lived in the front field was the worst of all. He would come into the front yard and wait for the little girl. Did he want to tell her something, or eat her? She never really knew. She would see him in the yard, every night, walking. When he would see her come out of the house, he would run for her, roaring, with white teeth bared. She would run back into the house, slamming the door shut. But she could hear him throw his weight against the wooden door. Would the door break apart? Would she live until morning? Every night she wondered if she would wake up in the sunlight again.

Eventually, I learned to make friends with that bear. I realized at last that he had things to tell me, and when I learned how to live with him, or at least how to survive that anger and rage that he represented, he never needed to roar again.

# Rage Reaction

I walked down the stairs from my bedroom, toward the front door. My jeans were brand new, and I had on a snazzy T-shirt and red tennis shoes. I was fourteen, and I planned to visit one of my friends in the neighborhood. I was excited to be going out.

From the right of the staircase, I heard my father bark out, "Where are you going?" He was in his favorite chair by the TV.

I looked straight ahead. "Out," I said. "I am going out."

"Where are you going?" he growled in a louder voice. I could sense him stand up. Out of the corner of my eye, my mother sat on the couch, her hands twisting and wringing in her lap. I kept walking.

"Goddamn it," he cursed. I heard him start to run for the stairs. I was only a few steps away.

I turned and bolted back the way I had come, instinctively running for the bathroom, which was the only room on that floor with a lock. I slid behind the door and turned the bolt. It was a small room, and the walls were a light purple tile. My best friend, Ann, whom I met after Pam had transferred to another school, loved those walls because they made her eyes look lavender, like Elizabeth Taylor's eyes.

He pounded on the flimsy door, trying to get in. It shuttered with every strike, and I cowered on the floor between the bathtub and toilet. The thin lock gave out, and he burst into the room. His black eyes burned like coal and several veins stuck out in his neck. I had never seen him so angry.

With his big hands, he jerked me to the floor by my neck and began to beat my head against the tiles. I felt the shock of the sharp blows against the left side of my head and face. I thought I was going to die.

From the hallway I heard a quiet voice. It was my mother. "John. John. John that could cause brain damage."

He brought my face up to his face. Inches away, his features were twisted out of shape—almost unrecognizable.

Suddenly he dropped me and stalked down the stairs loudly. My mother lingered by the door. Five feet tall, with her lime green apron on, she had a painful expression on her face. She was caught between the two of us—one of us cried on the bathroom floor while the other fumed in his favorite chair in the living room.

# Summer Vacation

During my childhood, we took yearly summer vacations to the Outer Banks. I think this was my dad's way of escaping to live on an island again, like he had as a kid in Puerto Rico. My parents were creatures of habit, and we always stayed at the same hotel in Kitty Hawk. This hotel was owned by an old white guy named Mr. C., with a booming voice, who loved my father and gave him the kingly treatment—the largest suite, overlooking the Atlantic Ocean. His wife, Mrs. C., with long silver braids that ran down her back, did the check-in and bookkeeping in between surf fishing for bluefish. She was quite a good fisherwoman, and we often ate fish on Friday nights, gathered around the wooden picnic tables in the park. She passed on when I was in my late thirties. During my childhood Mrs. C seemed invincible.

When I was an adult, my parents told me that Mr. C. had been her boss, and she was his secretary. They fell in love, and he left his wife for her—a betrayal or a romance, depending on whom you identify with. I always loved Mrs. C., but as an adult I identify more with the abandoned wife. I am surprised my proper Baptist mother let us stay there.

Dad was always happy at the Outer Banks. He was a different person when he was there. He was a nicer person at the beach. No angry outbursts, no hitting, just smiles and playfulness. He told a lot of puns and laughed a lot.

As his fishing buddy, I would go out with him at the crack of dawn to the local fishing pier. It was on a two-lane beach road, a ten-minute walk from where we stayed. Carrying our tackle, I would skip the entire way to the pier.

We would walk out to the very end of the pier, where four-foot sharks circled in the dark water below, and then drop our lines in the waves. We'd always make small talk with the guys who were on the pier.

"Nice weather."

"What is running today?"

"Caught anything?"

"Have you heard about the nor'easter due this weekend?"

I felt like one of the boys. At the end of the pier, the waves would lull me into a dream until mid-morning when we returned to wake up my mom, who had her own idea of a great vacation.

My mom liked to shop at the many mom-and-pop stores that lined the beach road with cheesy, hand-painted signs. Inside were shells with "North Carolina" painted on them, plastic-coated starfish, sand dollars, and awful T-shirts. I usually bought Superman comic books or *Mad Magazine,* though checkers sets, comic books galore, and piles of thick, glossy celebrity-gossip magazines beckoned. Mom would let me buy one thing for my entertainment.

We generally stopped for lunch at the strip of restaurants on the way to Manteo and the fishing village of Wanchese. (These towns were very small at the time, perhaps a hundred residents apiece.) We would order baskets of hush puppies, which smelled rich, and butter, and my father would make his joke about how hush puppies got their name. The bits of fried dough were thrown to hunting dogs to keep them quiet, hence the word "hush," for hush puppies.

# Pier Fishing

The desperate mullets struggle for
the edge of the wooden pier, gasping
for air. My father leans out over the
rail, casting his line beyond the
breakers. Flannel shirt and
army pants to protect him from the wind,
but the cold cuts through my light
jacket. A baseball cap pulled low
hides his dark face.
As his back is turned
I lay down my small rod and reel.
My hands tremble
as I strike, one blow to the head with
the blunt end of the knife, and
the fish lies quietly.

# A Heaping Helping of Fear and Guilt

The potlucks after church were full of fried foods and potatoes of all kinds. The fried chicken was so crispy and juicy that I still think of it when I go into that building, even though I no longer attend that church. But along with yummy chicken, the church served up a heaping helping of fear and guilt. We were all sinners in its eyes. We were going to hell if we were not "bathed in the blood of the lamb," and we sang hymns and read quotations from the Bible that illustrated that. The pastors taught us that the Bible was literal truth. God made the earth in seven days, and Eve was the origin of all our suffering on earth. And then, of course, there were the homosexuals and adulterers, who were too disgusting to be allowed to live.

It took me a long time to get over being afraid of hell. The panic attacks I felt at the thought of judgement day pervaded my adolescence. There were no choices that were not tinged by sin, and my main sins were talking back to my parents, being too proud, and acting unladylike.

Unfortunately, the chicken at home also came with a heaping helping of fear and guilt—guilt from the knowledge that I was never good enough for either parent. My mother was a Bible-thumper who often quoted scriptures with the verse number. Even doing the dishes was a battle between her and me. After I washed dishes and put them to dry, I'd come back later to find her rewashing the dishes, with a look of self-righteousness.

"There is a right way and a wrong way to do everything, M. J.," she'd say, as she redid my work.

"There are lots of ways to do things, Mom. There is no one right way," I told her as I stood by the sink. We were at an impasse.

With my father, things were worse. My fear at home was not about sin and hell in my eternal life but instead about explosions and anger in my current life. I never really knew what would set off my father. Once, he pointed a fork at my eye during lunch and told me, "I can take out your eye if I want to." He leaned across our small kitchen table, right there by my eyes, with a silver fork glinting in the afternoon sun.

    I don't serve arroz con pollo on Sundays anymore.

# Cherish

When I was fourteen, I knew I had feelings for Amanda, who had become my best friend after Pam left for high school. It happened one summer day as we listened to the song "Cherish" by The Association. on the radio, sitting on the floor of her grandparents' house. She sat with her long legs tucked underneath her, smiling. I was an awkward teenager, and so was she.

I am not sure why she was smiling, but for me, the song said it all. It was like the lyrics were speaking directly to me, even though I had no words to describe how I felt about her. The sixties were a time when there were no words for such feelings.

Growing up in the former capitol of the Confederacy, I felt alone and in the dark, but there she was, my best friend, and just as crazy as a June bug, with pent-up energy that expressed itself through running, jumping, laughing, and making decisions on the fly. We spent days at her grandparents' house in Varina. Amanda loved her ancient grandparents, and they treated me like one of the family. We spent sleepovers giggling over nothing and sleeping in her beautiful old four-poster bed with a picture of Robert E. Lee above the headboard.

We had lots of adventures together—everything we did felt like an adventure to me. Amanda introduced me to the hauntingly beautiful Hollywood Cemetery and the pyramid celebrating the fallen soldiers there. She would climb up the uneven stones of the pyramid, right to the top, which I thought was very daring. It was a very tall pyramid, and I felt afraid just watching her put one foot after another. I am sure she never told her mom about her tendency to climb the pyramid.

As for my own mom, she never understood the beauty of Hollywood Cemetery's ancient angels and holly-tree-lined walkways. "When you get closer to death yourself, cemeteries aren't so much fun," she warned me. My mom had been in her fifties at this point. She could already hear the clock ticking her life away, but for me, life had just begun.

One of the memorable points in my friendship with Amanda was when I turned fifteen and she came with my family on vacation to the

Outer Banks. My parents loved Amanda because she had such a good sense of humor. Amanda and I spent hours at the roller-skating rink, going around and around, or at the hotel, playing music, laughing, and reading teen magazines like *Tiger Beat*. We were always in motion, climbing sand dunes or chasing ghost crabs on the beach. My father even had a nickname for us, the "ghost crabs." After all that activity, we slept well at night.

Then we stopped calling each other suddenly. My mother tried to talk about it in a roundabout way when we were going on one of our afternoon rides.

"What happened between you and Amanda?" she asked me, looking out the corner of her eye as she steered the big green Chevrolet.

"I don't know, Mom," I answered as I stared out the window at the countryside rolling by.

"Well, it looks like you are brokenhearted."

"I don't know what you mean. What are you saying?" I answered quickly. I could feel myself turning red and starting to panic.

She turned her eyes back to the road. "It was just a thought."

"I don't know what you mean," I said again. I really didn't want to talk about it. It was too close for comfort.

Silence fell between us. She drove the car and I watched my life pass by me. It wouldn't be until college when I would finally have an answer to my conflicted thoughts in that moment.

# Goodbye

Grandmother Mary had left me when I was eight years old to live in a trailer in a field beside Uncle Clyde's house. The trailer had no plumbing or electricity, which was not that different from when she lived in our little house out back. The big difference was the cold weather in the mountains. It wasn't long before I heard that she was in the hospital. Was it pneumonia? No one told me the details. We went to visit her, and she was asleep when I saw her. She had a tube in her mouth to help with her breathing, and her color was all washed out. She looked small, old, and very alone. It was hard to look at the worn-down woman lying motionless in bed and recognize her as the same person I had stomped around Pocosham Creek with looking for fishing holes.

After that visit to the hospital, I never saw her alive again. I did not get a chance to say goodbye. I cried long and hard when I heard the news. My heart was broken. She was my ally and protector when I felt like I had no one else. I had wanted to be just like her when I grew up, and I thought she would be with me always. After her death, I slipped into a deep depression. Life felt dark and lonely. I didn't leave my room except to eat and go to school, and I learned to soothe my sorrow and loneliness with books. I read classics and lived mostly in my own imagination. I became Tom Sawyer, floating down the Mississippi River in *Adventures of Huckleberry Finn*. I devoured the Nancy Drew series and fell in love with *Alice in Wonderland*. Reading really did save my teenage years.

# The Day of the Dead

In a new body with
old eyes.

A sea of butterflies washes
over green mountains to find
this ancient graveyard. They
flutter on my shoulders
and barren tree branches.
Wise women have told me
these are loved ones,
traveling great distances to
caress my cheek.

# Coffee and Magnolias

Amazing how the tangy smell of Lucienne coffee makes
feelings rush over me like a high tide.
Love, loss, and joy, mixed with
cream and sugar in a cup.
Grandmother Mary loved her strong cup of coffee every morning.

I still have the beaten-up tin pot
she used to brew it in the little house.
I was so in love with her that I thought
the world had ended when she died.

Then there is the sweet smell of
magnolias,
which brings back memories of
Amanda
Running wild together in the front yard at
dusk. Chasing fireflies and laughing until
our sides hurt.
We lost each other when we were so young,
And now I wonder where you are.

# Then and Now

Floating layers,
surface warm,
ice-cold
at my feet. Suspended
in rivers, I linger
in the moment
then move on.

Grass grows here.
The platform lies
in pieces, crumbled.

# Part Two:

## *College and Coming Out*

(1970s, ages eighteen to thirty years old)

# Freedom

The year I graduated from high school was a year of chaos and change. My best friend, Katie, whom I grew close to after things ended with Amanda, had left with her family to move to Florida. I was heartbroken that she had also left me behind. I really didn't know if I was going to be able to make it through college without her. I had come to depend on talking with her on the phone and visiting her and her mom in their cute little green house, which was a fifteen-minute walk from my house. She and her mom made me feel as though I finally had a welcoming family, so their move felt very sudden. After they moved, her mother wrote me letters to stay in touch and support me. I was very depressed, and Katie was moping around her house, too. Her mother must have been worried about me because I found out later that she considered letting Katie move back to Richmond.

After high school, I enrolled at Virginia Commonwealth University because my parents expected me to go to college. I didn't care about anything at the time. Depression and grief will do that. I took the usual classes for a freshman: composition, philosophy, history, psychology, and religion. I found the masses of students at Hibbs Hall to be much more interesting than any of my classes. Kids in jeans and T-shirts, roller-skating and laughing together, congregating on the quad by the cafeteria. We were of different races and nationalities, but we were all trying to "find ourselves," and we all felt lost.

And then I started to pay more attention in my religion class. As a Baptist, the fear of damnation had been at the bottom of all actions in my life so far. The question was always, "What would Jesus do?" Then I read The Chronicles of Narnia by C. S. Lewis, which really changed my mind about how I could think and act. I decided to wear a buckskin jacket and blue jeans to church one Sunday and got lots of sidelong glances from the people in the pews. I knew I was about to walk down a new path.

My mother, of course, was not happy with my new path. I dropped out of college for a semester, cultivated a garden in the backyard, and drove up to Charlottesville to study Transcendental Meditation at a center there. This act was the final straw for my mother.

"M. J., we already have a religion," she warned me.

"Meditation is not a religion," I told her. "It is a spiritual practice."

She looked at me. "But we don't need it, do we?"

Charlottesville was an hour away from home, toward the Blue Ridge Mountains, which made spending lots of time at the Transcendental Meditation center a problem for me. One afternoon, while speeding down the interstate to get to a meditation meeting (ironic, I know), a cop stopped me for speeding. He shined his flashlight inside the car to see if I had drugs, probably because my long hair and jeans made me look like a hippie to him, even though everyone my age looked like that at the time. He gave me a ticket for reckless driving, and the court took away my driver's license for six weeks. That was the end of Transcendental Meditation meetings for me.

Even after that experience, I stayed very eclectic in my views, adopting whatever worked best for me from several philosophies. It was like the Al-Anon saying, "take what you like and leave the rest." I have found that meditation, Buddhism, New Age mysticism, and earth-based philosophies blend well for me and help me get in touch with that small, still voice in my head. That inner voice is the God part of the universe. I find it when I am still in my mind in meditation, or when I stay in contact with the energies of nature. This knowledge all started from that one fall semester when I discovered that there many paths to know God.

# Protests

I was eighteen years old and had just gotten my driver's license. The family car was my ticket to freedom. Even though I was still living at home, I felt free at last. Free to be out of my house. Free to be myself. Glorious, glorious freedom. I was off the chain and determined not to look back.

One Thursday afternoon, on the cement court between buildings where everyone hung out after classes, I heard that there would be a Vietnam War protest the next day in Washington, DC. This news was told to me by a long-haired, dirty-jeaned, torn-T-shirt-wearing guy, who was throwing a frisbee back and forth with his friends on the sidewalk between the buildings. During those days, there seemed to be two types of kids: the straight, church-going kids, who were Republican and Nixon-lovers, and the hippies. Richard Nixon called them "dirty hippies." He hated hippies and he hated protestors. I really didn't fit into either camp—I was in the middle of these groups—but I sided more with the hippies, so I decided to go to the protest.

I drove my beat-up white Chrysler to DC the next day, hoping to be able to find the protest easily, and I was right; it was easy. I parked the car and followed the sound of chanting down the street. The voices were very loud. The crowd was easy to find.

"Hey, hey, ho, ho, Nixon's got to go!"

"All we are saying is give peace a chance!"

I followed the mass of people moving peacefully down the street to an open area downtown and stood to listen to all the fiery speeches.

I felt very safe even though I didn't know anyone. People carried signs and passed out flowers as others mounted the stage to give passionate speeches. "These soldiers are being brought home in body bags!" one speaker shouted.

I read pamphlets with information ranging from the peace candidate, Eugene McCarthy, to the Students for a Democratic Society. Everyone I met wanted to talk to me about the peace movement. They were excited and friendly and very young. The sweet smell of marijuana drifted around us in the breeze as people passed homemade joints around. I felt swept up and carried along by the sea of passionate bodies.

But at the end of the day, I had a choice to make—everyone I met was going to "sleep in the park tonight."

"We will be safe," someone beside me offered. "There are hundreds of us. They can't arrest everyone."

The police had been a large presence during the march, but they had not interacted with the protestors in one way or the other. The men in blue had been neither friendly nor unfriendly. They had just been standing on the sidelines. But then I heard people mention cameras. "They are filming the crowd. They will start a file on you." I did not know what to think. I didn't want them to start a file on me.

Still, I did not think they could really arrest everyone who was sleeping in the park because *after all, this is America*, I thought, naive about what police presence might mean for protesters. But I still had this nagging piece of intuition going through my head. *Better go home now*, it said.

I followed this intuitive voice, thank goodness, and went back down the street, found my car, and drove home.

The next morning, in the *Richmond Times-Dispatch*, I read that they had arrested everyone in the park that night. They had herded them into a sports arena and booked them for trespassing on city property. I am sure there are still police files on the protesters who were caught, and I am extremely grateful to have missed the arrests.

# Iowa City

I escaped my parents and the South after one semester at VCU by enrolling in Parsons College in Iowa. It seemed like a good adventure at the time, and I was up for all adventures. Parsons was in the tiny town of Fairfield, Iowa. The school itself was in the middle of a cornfield, and Fairfield had a few stores, but that was it. I spent a lot of my time getting drunk with other students. One night I was so out of it that my friends had to carry me home to the dorm across the courtyard. It must have been quite a sight. I had been out at a party and this guy kept buying me drinks, hoping for a lucky night. I still didn't understand my sexuality at that point, and my friends had rescued me from him. I passed out in the dorm bathroom after throwing up, repeatedly. I woke up the next day, sprawled between the stalls, to the sounds of a janitor coming in to clean up the bathroom. I was so startled that I jumped up and stumbled to my room.

After a year at Parsons in Fairfield, I transferred to the University of Iowa in Iowa City. It was a hub of liberalism like I had never seen before. The University of Iowa was famous for the Iowa Writers Workshop. Many writers attended this famous writing program at the university, and Kurt Vonnegut was one of the lecturers. Even though I loved to write, I decided to be a psychology major. I chose that major to learn more about myself, and to please my father, who wanted me to choose a "practical" major. In hindsight, I probably should have chosen a creative writing major. I had always loved to write, but I gave in to my parents' choice for me.

At the University of Iowa, I continued to party hard, just like the other students around me. My drug of choice was alcohol, but there certainly were other choices I could have made. I tried marijuana once but decided that the feeling of being out of control when high, as opposed to being out of control when drunk, was not for me. I am glad I never tried LSD. Even then, there were stories about people who were high on LSD jumping out of windows because they thought they could fly. Sometimes it was very hard to get up for my eight a.m. classes, but I made myself do it.

I lived in the dorms that were up the street from the campus buildings. There was always something going on in our hallway. My room was the party room, and it was not unusual for me to come back from classes to find people hanging out, waiting for me. My roommate, Paula, didn't like all the noise and drinking, but she was overruled by everyone else.

Iowa City is where I met many lifelong friends. Cindy and Sharon, who lived in the room at the end of the hall, saw something in me that I had not realized was there. They started giving me books to read like *Rubyfruit Jungle* and *Patience and Sarah*. These books about women loving women were a game changer for me. Was this kind of attraction really an option?

At the time there was not a lot of accessible information about gay people. Our desires and attractions were still a secret to the larger population, and sometimes to ourselves, too. Gay people routinely married the expected gender and stayed in the closet their entire lives, longing for something else. I should automatically have known I had feelings for women, but being exposed to the stories of other gay people opened the closet door just enough for me to look out and see new things.

I was curious, so my new friends Cindy and Sharon took me to dances that were held in the basement of the local Unitarian Church. In the cozy, dark room, women danced with other women. I stood on the sidelines, gaping in awe.

One day, Cindy and Sharon said they knew someone who might come with me to one of these dances. I said yes, but I was scared. When my date, Patricia, pulled up to the dorm in her sports car, my heart fell out of my chest. Her long brown hair swung as she got out of the car and walked up the sidewalk. I waited inside the dorm door. *Wow* was all I could think.

Patricia and I drove down the street to Joe's Inn for a beer and some conversation. We were talking about surface level stuff, like college majors and the music we liked, when I noticed my friends had followed us to the bar and snuck past our booth. It was like a scene from a comedy—they were curious too. They couldn't wait for me to get back to the dorm to find out how it was going. It tuns out, things were going very well.

At the dance, Patricia reached up and grabbed one of the silver stars that decorated the ceiling. It was just a star made of cardboard and wrapped in tin foil, but it felt like so much more. We danced the night away to Donna Summer, and I knew she would become a big part of my life.

# Coming Out

I was very lucky to have been able to come out in the early seventies. If I had been in my twenties in the fifties or sixties, a generation before mine, I would have had to endure living in the closet, because that would have been my only option. I would have had to meet people at night in dark bars, never acknowledging the true nature of our relationships. Friends. Roommates. That's how life was all over the US in the mid-twentieth century. In the seventies, we had more options, due to new laws, feminism, and the gay liberation movement.

In Iowa City in the seventies, I had more options. There was a women's center across the street from the student commons that held support groups for women who were coming out. There was also the Gay Liberation Front, a national organization that helped gay people to accept themselves, that was active in Iowa City. The Gay Liberation Front had not been active in Richmond, although there was a women's center there. In terms of community in Richmond, there were two somewhat openly gay bars to play pool and dance, and the rest of the bars were gay-friendly—women dancing together would have been no big deal. On the national level, there was a new magazine called *Off Our Backs* that published articles about feminism and lesbianism.

And then, of course, there was softball. In the Midwest, softball is the most important event of the summer, and the lesbian community had our own all-lesbian teams to watch. I spent countless summers evenings watching softballs fly and listening to the crack of the bat and the cheers from the audience, who were crowded onto metal bleachers. I loved it. And I knew everyone in the stands. The gay community in Iowa City was a small community, and we knew each other well.

Iowa City had recently passed a gay rights ordinance, and we were protected from discrimination there. We could not be fired or turned out into the streets from our apartments just for being gay or lesbian. Iowa City was very forward thinking for the seventies. My hometown of Richmond would not enact a law like this until 2020.[1]

---

[1] "Bill Tracking – 2020 Session," Virginia's Legislative Information System, LIS, April 11, 2020, https://lis.virginia.gov/cgi-bin/legp604.exe?201+ful+CHAP1137.

Though I felt welcomed by the gay community in Iowa City, I had other issues with coming out. I wish my love-at-first-sight beginning with Patricia had stayed that ideal, but it didn't. There were problems from the start of the relationship. To begin with, we lived in different towns. She lived in a larger working-class town, thirty minutes away from me. Since I was in college, this put a strain on my ability to go to classes. My eight o'clock classes quickly became a terrible chore since I frequently slept over at Patricia's place.

Things were also complicated by Patricia's other relationships. She had been living in the country with her boyfriend, Jason, when she started to question her sexuality. He told her to go and find out what she really wanted. I suspect he had no idea that she would meet someone else. Jason was torn. He wanted her to be happy, but he had a hard time letting her go. This put a terrible strain on our relationship.

I also couldn't tell what was going on with my own feelings. I couldn't escape my southern roots, and I really wanted to settle down and get married. This desire to marry was at odds with my peers' feelings—marriage was considered incredibly old-fashioned at the time. Many people, gay and straight, were experimenting with non-monogamous relationships, and there was a lot of peer pressure to have an open relationship.

After a rocky year together, Patricia and I broke up. That summer, I got together with Dorothy. Dorothy was the opposite of Patricia; she was not flashy, and she seemed to want to settle down. I was happy with her, but as luck would have it, in the fall, Patricia told me she wanted to get back together.

This was the start of all three of us living together. It started with just me and Dorothy living together, then the three of us living together in a small house in a tiny country town, and then Patricia and Dorothy getting involved romantically while I still lived with them. Eventually, we all split up. After our tumultuous time living together, Dorothy got into a car accident, and I went to visit her.

When I saw her in the hospital, I was wracked with remorse. I wanted to get back together with her because I thought she was the best person for me. I asked for Patricia's advice before I talked to Dorothy, and Patricia advised against it, so I let the moment pass. In hindsight, this was a terrible mistake. I should have talked to Dorothy. She would have been a good choice for me to settle down with as she was calm and level-headed.

Patricia and I got back together for another year after Dorothy's accident, and then we parted ways. The anger and betrayal I felt toward her at the end of our relationship was intense. She had continued to see other people while we were dating, and I wish we had both said it was time to part ways sooner. Our relationship ended with a bad scene outside of an out-of-town bar where I tried to throw a drunken punch at her and ended up landing on the concrete instead. The news of our drama traveled to Iowa City on the lesbian telephone express, and I had to listen to everyone's opinion about it as I sat watching softball the next day. The votes were fifty-fifty on my actions. Some thought I was a horrible person, and others thought she may have deserved it. But what mattered most to me was how I felt—embarrassed and disgusted that I had acted just like my father.

# Mom

Coming out to my mother back in Richmond was not as easy as coming out in Iowa City had been. I started hinting that a change was coming by going from long hair to short hair. It was a truly short haircut, and I loved running my fingers through it to comb it. But my mother was not as thrilled with it. And then I added boots and army jackets to my style. These kinds of clothes were in fashion among my new friends but weren't as fashionable in Richmond. It was still conservative as a city, and I didn't know any lesbians. One Christmas, I took the bus home and got off in my army jacket, boots, and baseball hat, carrying my clothes in a paper bag. My mother came over to me and said, "It really hurts your father to see you looking like this."

On the way to pick up dad from work, she asked me the question that was on her mind.

"Mattie Jo, do you like women?"

I didn't exactly know what she meant so I said, "Yes, Mom, women are wonderful."

She replied, "No, I mean do you like them? Are you a 'lesbon'?"

I didn't know whether to laugh or cry, "Yes, Mom, and the word is 'lesbian.'"

"Well, what is it that you do?" she said. I knew she meant sexually. This was a question I never wanted to talk about with my mom. I gave a brief description, and she responded, "Well, don't tell your father."

Though she forbade me from doing so, I think she ended up telling him herself because soon after that, they both stopped asking when I would be getting married. They stopped asking me questions about relationships altogether. Even though I brought Patricia home often to visit for holidays, and my dad seemed to really love her, no one dared to ask any questions. If we didn't talk about it, then they didn't have to face it—a "maybe it will just go away" kind of strategy.

# Haunted in Solon

I remember the first time I saw our house outside of Solon, Iowa. The doors and shutters were sitting wide open, and junk was piled up on the back porch. The house looked sad, and I thought to myself, *Dear God, what are we getting into here?*

I had driven to the house, which was forty-five minutes from town, with Patricia in her little black Honda Civic. We were deep in the country, surrounded by fields of cattle and sheep, and on a one-lane gravel road. Patricia had heard about the house from George, one of her coworkers at a factory she worked at in Iowa City. I was still in college at this point, and we were both in our early twenties, broke and looking for a bargain. It had not occurred to me yet that the saying "you get what you pay for" was true.

"George says it hasn't been lived in for many years. It used to be a party house for hippies," Patricia explained. "Lots of drugs and alcohol and all that."

"I'll bet it's true. It has a weird vibe to it," I answered.

"Let's see what it looks like inside," she suggested as she parked the car. We walked up the driveway and through the tall grass in the front yard. The house was white with two stories, a side porch, and windows that looked out onto the road. We went up to the porch door and it opened easily with a loud creaking sound. We both stood still.

"Hello, hello, is anyone there?" I called inside. The door opened into a dusty kitchen. There were no footprints on the floor, and it looked like no one had been in the kitchen for a very long time. We stepped inside slowly. Downstairs, there was a living room and two bedrooms, all of which were empty. Upstairs we found a large open room. The thud of our steps on the floor echoed in the empty house.

As we walked out of the porch door, Patricia asked me, "Well, what do you think?"

I had a creepy feeling that someone was watching me as I left. I turned around to look over my shoulder. No one was there.

"I don't know," I said quietly.

"I know, let me think about it."

We closed the door, walked back to the car, and drove off down the rutted gravel road.

As we drove back to Iowa City, Patricia convinced me this would be a good idea, so we began our move our things to the country. At this point, Patricia and I had been living in a tiny apartment at the corner of Dubuque and Brown Streets in Iowa City. It took us several car trips to get into the house. I drove a truck, which helped with our move, but the new house was twenty miles away, and it took time and money to get there. Stereos, records, books, clothes, and mismatching dishes and cups jostled around the back as we drove down the road to the house. Later, Dorothy moved into the house in Solon with us.

One afternoon, as I sped past an open field, I noticed a man walking with a rifle in the sunlight. I looked away from him to change the channel on the radio, and when I looked back in the rearview mirror, his image was gone. It sent a chill through me.

Fall turned to winter. We had moved and settled into the downstairs portion of the house, but the upstairs remained empty. As the days went on, things that had been fine between the three of us started to become strained, and the isolated location of the house was certainly no help. Patricia and I began to argue a lot, and Dorothy, being another twenty-something-year-old, played us against each other. We argued about money, college, and playing music too loud. I started playing Elton John's album *Goodbye Yellow Brick Road* twenty-four hours a day. I drank beer and danced in the living room.

One night, as Patricia and I were bickering in the kitchen while making dinner, we both heard a thud on the ceiling.

"What was that?" I whispered.

"I don't know," she replied.

Another thump landed on the ceiling right above us.

"Something doesn't like us," I said.

There came another clunk on the ceiling as we looked up in disbelief. We went silent. A few days before, the first snowstorm of the season had blanketed the countryside in white and stranded us in the house. Patricia had had a vivid dream, and she had woken me up to tell me about it. In the dream, she had heard music coming from upstairs and the sound of people dancing. She had been certain that couples were dancing together over our heads. Her experience had been so vivid that now, we both went upstairs to see if there were footprints in the dust. There were no footprints.

A few days later, on one of my frequent journeys through the countryside, I had stopped at a family graveyard. I had noticed that the cornerstone on our house said, "Evans, 1914," and I was very curious about who had lived there before us. I looked at the names and dates on the small gravestones. Stone after stone had the date 1914 carved into it as the date of death.

Then I saw it. The name "Evans" was etched on a plain headstone. Beloved wife, beloved husband, and two children under the age of two were all buried there and had died in the same year. A cold chill came over me as I stood in this country cemetery. Was I living in a house where the previous owners had refused to leave when they died? Had they moved upstairs instead of going toward the light?

That idea should have been enough to get us to move. The final straw came for me during a December snowstorm. Patricia and Dorothy were in Iowa City, and I was snowed in alone at the house, watching the snowflakes coming down through the living room window. It was a beautiful snow that covered the ground and my car in a blanket of white.

While I was admiring the snow, I thought I heard the footsteps upstairs again. I knew instinctively that someone was in the house with me, even though there were no tire tracks in the driveway or footprints in the snow. I had to get out.

I started up my truck, packed my belongings into the backseat, and slowly drove twenty miles to Iowa City during the snowstorm. I never went back to that house—Dorothy and Patricia went back to clean out the belongings that were left. The house sat empty for years after we left it.

# Tiffin

The next house that Patricia, Dorothy, and I rented was much quieter. It was in a small town called Tiffin, just west of Iowa City. The population of the town was under a hundred, and it had a high school, grocery store, and bar. The whole town was north of a set of railroad tracks. Tiffin was so small that during fall, the king and queen of homecoming would ride down the only two streets in town and wave to the residents, who would crowd the streets to cheer them on. Even I went outside of the house to wave back.

The sisters who rented the house to us were happy to have us there. We paid regular rent, and that was all they asked of us. The residents of the town, however, were a different matter.

We had a doghouse for Butch, the very large dog we had just bought. Butch was a brown-and-white Great Dane mix and very friendly. The doghouse was very heavy, and when we were bringing it home, we managed to drop it in the yard, and it rolled into the street. Later that day someone from across town came over to greet us, and she mentioned the rolling doghouse. The rolling doghouse and the mysterious college girls were tantalizing news that had traveled through the town in just a few hours.

But the biggest town gossip was a teenager in a wheelchair who lived just across the street. He had binoculars and a curiosity about college girls. He kept his binoculars trained on our house for the duration of the year we lived there. He would give updates about us to his mother, who would then get on the phone with her friends. Our lives were normal for college kids, with lots of parties and drinking. Nothing really wild, but still, it was news for folks in town.

While we lived in Tiffin, I would walk down the street a lot to drink beer and shoot pool at the local bar in town. I was one of the regulars there. My biggest moment of pride was when I beat one of the local men at a game of pool. I was very proud of that accomplishment since the bar-goers took their pool games very seriously. They played all the time together and were highly skilled. The man I beat did not take his defeat at pool by a woman very well and stormed out of the bar to walk home.

# Monica

After I graduated college, I decided to move to Phoenix, Arizona. I had broken up with both Patricia and Dorothy, Butch had been rehomed, and the thought of living in the West was exciting. Ultimately, I found Phoenix to be too conservative, and I left after six months, moving back to Iowa City. I returned to the crisis center where I had worked during college—it was a group I knew and loved. The crisis center was a group of volunteers and two staff members who ran a food center and hotline for any emergency calls. It was a perfect fit for me because helping people gave me a sense of purpose. The people who worked there wanted to make a difference in the world. Kevin, the director, and Sue, the assistant director, were both warm and loving people. Except for Kevin, who was the old guy of the group at forty, we were all in our twenties.

I returned to my old job as a trainer for the new volunteers. I had done this before and was very comfortable with the job. We did trainings twice a year in the basement of the Unitarian church, with twenty to thirty trainees in each training course. The center ran through volunteers quickly because it was so stressful to work there—we never really knew who would be calling or knocking on the door—but I liked the adrenaline rush I got from working there. The sense of danger reminded me of the volatile atmosphere of my childhood when I never knew when Dad would start yelling and screaming. At the crisis center, we never knew when something would erupt in the town and would need our intervention. It was a constant adrenaline rush.

In my first few months after returning to Iowa City, I met a woman in the newest group of recruits named Monica. She was short and had a cute smile. She and I became friends while I trained her, and then we started to date. She was curious about the lesbian lifestyle.

Soon after Monica and I started to date, Sue left the assistant director role, and I took her place. It was the job of a lifetime for me, my first full-time job after college, and I was filled with purpose. It didn't matter to me that I seldom had time to take a lunch break, or that when I did grab a sandwich, I often found myself running across the parking lot to jump in my car and go to the hospital for an emergency call. I was short on time. Adrenaline was my middle name. I didn't sleep well because when I wasn't on call at night, my brain would be replaying the day's activities in a loop. Once, I remember taking a phone call right after I woke up from a deep sleep, from a woman crying because she had been raped.

In the middle of this intense mix, Monica moved in with me. My house was a two-story, old, green, wooden house with a large front porch, only three blocks from my work. My relationship with Monica had been very up-and-down from the start. It was either wonderful or it was awful, with no in-between. After she moved in, I continued to not sleep well, and sometimes at night, I would cry so hard that tears filled my ears. After some time together, Monica began to question whether she wanted a bisexual lifestyle after all. We started to argue—about food and rent. Neither of us had a lot of extra money. Once, I gave her a turquoise pinky ring and a little, gray, stray kitten. The kitten got sick and died. Monica took that death to be a sign that things were not going to get better between us.

The week before Valentine's Day, I came home from work and found the ring I had given her on the sofa with a note that said goodbye. All her things were gone. During the day, she had moved everything out with some help from her friends. I was devastated. Her last comments to me had been, "I love you, but I am not in love with you." She had decided to not live a bisexual lifestyle, and she was rejecting me totally.

It was very hard for me to continue my day-to-day activities, but I managed to hold it together. A few months after she left, I started to feel better. Then I began to hear gossip. Monica had stayed at the crisis center and was working night shifts. She was talking to her fellow volunteers about me, and not in a good way, sharing things we had fought about before she left. These conversations were getting back to me. I left her a message that I wanted to talk with her, but she wrote me a note back to say that she didn't want to talk. Eventually it became obvious the gossip wasn't going to stop. The criticism was devastating, so I turned in my resignation to Kevin. He kept it on his desk for a week without acting on it, I think in hopes I would change my mind. But I didn't change my mind—I packed my things from the office and left my first job, full of pain and regret.

# The Longest Winter

It all started with Monica's February departure, a few days before Valentine's Day. I had an accident in the parking garage coming home from work. I slipped on a sheet of black ice while going back to my car. I didn't see it, and I slid on the cement very hard. I was by myself. My right knee popped out of joint, and I had to push the kneecap back into the right place on my leg.

After Monica left, I moved out of the house we had lived in and bought a trailer in a park that was south of town. It was a nice trailer park, filled with families and kids. I thought I was making a good investment, not understanding that trailers lose their value quickly.

My life felt like one big crisis. I was thirty years old, and it was the middle of February in Iowa. I had a right leg that wouldn't heal, and a broken heart that wasn't healing well, either. I wasn't thinking straight. I would lie on the couch in the trailer, watch the snow falling, and feel very dark inside. I spent a lot of time in the trailer brooding. Luckily, I had gotten a black cocker spaniel named River and a Siamese cat named Boomer after I moved back from Phoenix, and they kept me company.

Weeks went by, and finally the weather started to break. I was feeling better, and my heart was on the mend. I heard a knock on the door, and it was my friend Marilyn. Usually Marilyn was very funny, but she wasn't laughing on that day.

"Monica is getting married soon," she told me.

"What?"

"Yes, she is getting married. I wanted to be the one to tell you. I didn't want you to read about it in the paper."

She stood there and waited for a reaction. I was stunned and sat down. I didn't know what to say. Monica and I had just broken up six weeks before. Neither Marilyn nor I knew what to say. I looked out the window of my trailer and all I saw was grayness.

That day, I got a letter from my mother begging me to come home. It was one of her usual letters, but it caught me at just the right time. I packed up my bags and my pets and put them in my car. Most of my important belongings were in the trunk, and I had put all my furniture into a storage unit, expecting to return after a visit. In my mind this trip was just a visit to Mom and Dad. Little did I know how complicated that trip home would be. I had never planned to return to Richmond for good, but I soon found out the situation at home was bad, as my mom was showing signs of dementia and needed my help.

My knee had still not totally healed, and it was almost impossible for me to use my right leg to drive. I had been using a cane to walk, and I used it to press on the accelerator. It was painful and difficult. It took me two solid days of eight-hour turnpike-driving to make it out to Virginia. River was in the front, riding shotgun. Boomer sat in the back seat with her litter pan, crawling up the back window and howling the entire trip. She was not a happy camper. We stayed in a cheap hotel one night and traveled from dawn until dusk.

When my cross-country drive was finished and I hobbled up to the house on my cane, both parents were surprised. I was clearly in bad shape. In hindsight, they were both probably thinking, *We've got you now*. I was thinking, *This isn't good*.

# Part Three:

*Coming Home*

(1980s and 1990s, ages thirty to fifty years old)

# Healing

Even though I thought my trip home would be a short one, I ultimately decided it was best to stay in Richmond to help my mother. I moved into a rental house that was owned by a broken-up lesbian couple, not far away from my family home, and took on two part-time jobs. One of my jobs was selling silver New Age jewelry to bookstores on consignment. It was beautiful jewelry and very easy to sell. My second job was as a counselor at a small college. It was hard to make ends meet even with two jobs.

At the time, the gay bars in town were restaurants by day and bars at night. There was always the threat of a police raid because it was against the law to sell alcohol to a "known homosexual." There was even one bar that had a bouncer at the door to look you over before letting you in.

The big place to meet was softball at Humphrey Calder Park. The bleachers were always packed for the Friday night games. Many of the players were lesbian, but they didn't advertise the teams in that way. After the game we would go to Babes, a lesbian bar, to dance and play pool. The other women at Babes were very serious pool players, just as the bar-goers at the small-town bars in the Midwest had been. The big difference, of course, is that if you win a game against another woman, they won't storm out, insulted. They might even like it and ask for your phone number. At Babes, there was karaoke and all kinds of dance contests. It was such a great place to spend a Friday night that I was tempted to become one of the cool bartenders there.

But I soon found that Richmond in the eighties was a lot like Richmond in the sixties. I had assumed that my ten years away would have meant that Richmond caught up with the rest of the country, but I was wrong.

Richmond had originally been built on seven hills, like Rome. But unlike Rome, each of those seven hills had a separate character based on economics and race. The East End, Churchill, and Fulton were the original center of town but had fallen into disrepair and poverty. The new center of town, with the Capitol Building and VCU Medical Center, was thriving. The area around VCU, the Fan, was also in disrepair. The North Side, by Bryan Park, was where the middle-income families lived. The West End, by the University of Richmond, was a high-income area, full of mansions and oak-lined streets—you could smell the money that had been inherited, or made in law, medicine, or the stock market, as you drove through. Then there was Southside, which was the area south of the James River. It was a rural area when I was growing up, and then it was annexed to the city and became more working-class. My family's patch of the area still felt rural. Across the road from my parents' house was an older home that flew a Confederate flag, and when I was growing up, "Dixie" was played on the radio every morning. My own family was multicultural, but we never went to the Thalhimers lunch counter, where they had the protests in 1960, and when I wanted to bring black friends home, I was told gently, "I don't think so."

Anti-gay and anti-lesbian attitudes were as obvious as racist attitudes. In grade school, calling someone a "queer" was considered a terrible insult. As a teenager I remember seeing the word "queer" painted on the rocks in our creek, which made my father very upset. Even I used the word without exactly knowing the meaning. Once, I went with a bunch of kids to write "queer" in soap on a classmate's picture window. Our classmate turned on the porch light and waved to us as we scrambled away into the darkness.

Even though it still felt like the Richmond of my childhood, there were acts of what felt like bravery in the eighties. There was a print version of the *Richmond Lesbian Feminist Flyer*, which I volunteered for. There was also the first gay pride parade, which met at the Carillon and marched a short distance down the street. We all knew each other, and there were hundreds of happy gay people and their allies walking down the street for justice.

In Richmond in the eighties, the out-and-proud community was small, but the closeted community was probably very large. I experienced this dichotomy myself when I briefly dated a college professor. It felt like a reasonable choice for a relationship since she was a friend who loved animals and books, as I did. But she ended things with me after she had a dream that she would be denied tenure because of our relationship.

When I became an English teacher, I didn't keep my sexuality a secret, but I wasn't open about it either. No one asked me who I was dating, and there were no pictures of women on my desk at work. My hair was short, and I never wore dresses.

One year, the school decided to have a tree planting ceremony to honor veterans outside of a building on the new campus. I lined up behind all the men, since I was the only woman who felt comfortable with a shovel, to throw a shovel full of dirt into the hole where this tree was to live. The older, very southern school president looked at me as though it was very strange that I could handle a shovel.

Gender roles have always been fluid for me. I wore pants and had short hair even in the fifties, when southern women were expected to act like belles. I had always been more interested in being a boy scout, rather than a girl scout. Boy scouts got to do cooler things, after all—camping and fishing trips, as opposed to bake sales and selling cookies. I fit in much better in college when I went to the Midwest. The Midwest has a history of farm girls working on the land, and I could fit in there. But in Richmond, the expectation for every woman was to be like Scarlett O'Hara, with her iron fist in a gloved hand. Duality, not continuum, was the norm then.

# Jennifer

She came back into my life without a warning. After moving back to Richmond, I was reintroduced to Jennifer. One of my current friends said she knew one of my childhood friends through playing golf, and did I want to contact her? Of course, I did. When we met for coffee at Starbucks, I knew her immediately. Jennifer was my friend from grade school at a small private school in the country. She had been put into private school by her parents because she was deaf and needed extra support. But she felt like it was a punishment. I had been put there by my parents to escape public school (and probably integration), but it felt like a punishment to me, too.

When I look back at the film my father took at the May Day event at that school, I am struck by how miserable I look. I had been voted one of the May queens and was onstage with a fresh haircut and a frilly blue dress. I felt and looked like a prisoner of war.

I begged to be taken out of this school because I was bullied for my interest in sports. Jennifer was bullied too—because she was deaf. My parents did not listen to me, and Jennifer's parents were also deaf to her pleas to leave that school. She and I exchanged pinky rings in the sixth grade, and I have kept mine in a jewelry box all my life.

Jennifer was a year younger than me and was there when the school became a high school. I had escaped after sixth grade because there weren't any grades beyond that, and went to a public high school, which I loved. At the end of high school, Jennifer's parents chose a husband for her from her classmates.

Jennifer and I lost touch until decades later when we had that coffee in Starbucks. Jennifer had gone to nursing school and come out as a lesbian after divorcing the husband that her parents had chosen for her. She and I hadn't met as adults in Richmond even though it was a very small lesbian community at the time. We were running in separate circles but leading parallel lives. She was a golfer, and I was a social activist who marched for abortion rights, the ERA, and gay rights, and apparently those groups did not overlap in Richmond at the time.

Jennifer had discovered she had leukemia a year before we reconnected. She looked healthy and had lots of energy and friends. It was tempting for me to think she would be okay, but her hospital trips to the Medical College of Virginia for transfusions became more frequent. She was always upbeat, but she did tell me one evening, over dinner at Jason's Diner, that she could feel "life slipping away" from her. I tried to console her and tell her that wasn't the case, but she was right.

We only had two wonderful years of knowing each other again before she became gravely ill. By the end of her life, the blood vessels in her face were breaking down, which gave her a greenish glow. On my last visit with her before her death, she had been taking a nap on her couch. When I came in, she woke up, and said to me, "I saw an indigo light." I told her that indigo light was very spiritual. It represents the light that connects us to the universe. She gave me her deck of Animal Spirit tarot cards in a beautiful box with horses on the front. She told me that when she died, she would be happy because she "would be in heaven and be able to hear." This was the last time I saw her alive.

But after she died, I caught a glimpse of her during her celebration of life ceremony, in the left-hand corner of the Unitarian church we both attended, and to which I had started going in the mid-eighties. I had a strong vision of her there. She looked young and vibrant like when she was a young girl. She had written the ceremony herself and was clearly having a great time watching it unfold. She was smiling and laughing. When I told her, in my thoughts, that I would miss her, the vision of her ran over to me and gave me a hug before she disappeared for her next life in heaven.

# Summer Festivals

For many years the Richmond Lesbian Feminists, an organized group with a newsletter and meetings, went on a summer retreat to the cabins at Pocahontas State Park. The organization was small, and we all knew each other. These retreats weren't large gatherings, and there would be maybe one hundred people in attendance. We would bring only food, a change of clothes, and bed sheets in our backpacks and would stay in rustic cabins like summer camp kids. I loved it. Everyone there was either friends, friends with a past, or friends with benefits. At night, a DJ would play music in the main dining hall. I love to dance. I would dance by myself or with groups of women. Sometimes I danced without my shirt, which always felt so wild and free.

One of the festivals the local lesbians would try to attend each summer was the Michigan Women's Festival. The festival was held every year, but I only managed to travel there for the festivities one summer in the early eighties. It was huge, with a thousand women in attendance, and incredibly peaceful. The summer I attended, I drove up in my little black truck with just my tent. I ate only vegetarian food and listened to women's music from Meg Christian, Holly Near, and Cris Williamson—bands I had only heard on records—performing live, right there on stage at night. It was incredible. No fights or squabbling. Just peace and love.

I must also admit that I have never been a good tent camper. My idea of roughing it has always included cabins or campers. In Michigan, it got cold at night, even in the summer. I remember being so cold, the frigid air forced me out of my tent to wander the paths, looking for heat. I ended up huddling with other campers around a roaring campfire. It looked and felt like the end of the world—bonfires set by the survivors of Armageddon, searching for warmth and the company of other humans as we planned how to get through the next days of the new world.

Being among my peers felt glorious, and at the Michigan Women's Festival, I felt safe from harassment and free to be exactly who I was. No pretense. No leaving out details. Just having fun. I wished this experience could go on forever. When I got back to Virginia, I considered the possibility of joining the local hippie community of Twin Oaks—a wonderful artistic community that supported itself with handmade hammocks. The only problem was that no cats or dogs were allowed, and that was a deal breaker for me.

# Things Unsaid

I don't remember my father ever telling me he was proud of me. When I was a counselor, he used to drop by work unannounced and just hang out with me. He looked happy, and I guess that was pride. He often told me I should stay at my job because "it was a good, steady state job." I guess that was pride. I really don't know.

I don't ever remember Dad telling me he was sorry for any of the things he did. He yelled, he screamed, he hit me in the face, but not once did he express remorse.

I don't remember Dad telling me he loved me. He bought me little silver horses and horse head bookends because I loved horses, but he never asked what I might like.

Mom told me how much she loved me a lot and once confided in me over lunch that she wished she could have traveled all over the country "like I did." But just below the surface of the love was "I need you. I can't live without you. Don't ever leave me." I don't know if this feeling had to do with her relationship with my father or not, but these underlying messages made me feel trapped. I think part of this was her own depression. When I asked her what she wanted to do together, she never looked happy or expressed an interest in doing anything, except eating banana splits. Trips to the ice cream store would make her smile, but not much else seemed to affect her. It looked to me like she was living in a pit full of gloom. I stood on the edge of the hole she lived in and tried to talk with her. If she was having a very bad day, she would tell me, "I wish you had never been born."

When I was a kid, we all lived in separate worlds. Dad's world was work and being an "Important Doctor." Mom's world was cats, dogs, and me. My world was books, cats, dogs, and horses. I don't remember being taken care of or protected after the age of ten. That was the year my grandmother died in the hospital alone.

# Alzheimer's

I realized things were not right with my mother when she leaned over to me and whispered, "I don't appreciate you telling people I am cheating on your father." I was home from college, and I went ballistic—what she had said was so ridiculous and obviously imaginary. I started yelling and told her to "get away from me." Something was very wrong. This was not the mother I had known all my life.

After I came back from Iowa City, I knew things were bad when Mom forgot how to cook the turkey for Thanksgiving. She had been a fantastic cook, and Thanksgiving was her special day, but as we all stood in the kitchen trying to help, she couldn't remember how to do anything. The fantastic cook couldn't even safely turn on the stove. I got Chinese takeout for us with a feeling of dread in the pit of my stomach.

There were other warning signs that illness was about to take over her life, and mine too. She began hiding things under the cushions of the couch for "safekeeping." She would get lost driving in places she had known for decades. I became a parent to my mother just as certainly as she had been a parent to me. I worked two part-time jobs as a jewelry salesperson and a college counselor by day and then watched Mom at night to relieve the certified nursing assistants who took care of her. My dad helped too, but mostly, he and I supervised the workers. I felt overwhelmed all the time.

We finally hired a full-time CNA, but she was a mixed blessing because she came with her own weird agenda. She really wanted to start her own nursing care business at my family home, after mom was gone. I am not sure how she expected her idea to work, as she clearly did not have money to buy a house. Maybe she thought Dad would give her the house in return for sex. Dad would regularly sexually proposition her, and she would tell me about it. I was appalled, both for her and also for my mother. How could he be that gross?

One night in the kitchen I heard him yelling at my mother upstairs in her bedroom. I ran up the stairs two at a time and saw him about to backhand her as she lay trapped in her hospital bed with aluminum railings to keep her safe.

I screamed, "No!" and held my hand out in a signal to stop. I felt like a faithful black lab rushing to help her mistress. I was determined to save her.

He looked over at me in the doorway, hand still up in the air, face full of fury. Then he dropped his hand and shoved past me to go down the stairs to the living room. I stood by my mother's bed for a long time, guarding her, after he left. I sobbed great tears of agony. My relationship with my mother had always been difficult, but I would be damned if I stood by and watched a blind woman being beaten up in bed. No. Not on my watch.

At the end of her life, we brought my mother's hospital bed downstairs to the dining room, replacing the table that was there. A week before she died, she started to have whole conversations with Grandmother Mary and Uncle Clyde. She had been very close to her brother Clyde, and she asked him how he was doing and told him how much she missed him. She said all this while looking up at the right-hand corner of her room. I could picture Mary and Clyde floating up there, talking quietly with her. By this time, she had gone totally blind from macular degeneration, but she seemed to see them right there in the room with her. I have no doubt they were there in the room. Her loved ones had come to take her into the light, into heaven.

# Drinking

When my dad died in the hospital of congestive heart failure, it was a shock. I think it was probably a shock for him too. He was eighty years old and still a good-looking man, but one day he just fell back in bed after eating lunch and flirting with the nurses and passed away.

So much was left unanswered. Had he loved my mother? Had he loved me? He had survived two years longer than my mother, and I honestly thought he was planning to remarry and have a second act to his story. One of his girlfriends contacted me after his death to tell me that was the case.

Cleaning out his room at home was eye-opening for me. As I cleared out his wardrobe, I found bottles of half-consumed brown liquid in between rows of hanging sweaters. In his chest of drawers were more half-empty bottles reeking of strong liquor. He had even hidden bottles of whiskey in the little house where my grandmother had lived.

This was all a shock to me since I had never seen my father drunk. I felt sick to my stomach. I think now people would call my father a functional alcoholic. They say that hiding alcohol is a sign of alcoholism. Normal drinkers don't usually stash away alcohol in secret places.

Perhaps he was self-medicating to deal with his problems. I am sure there are multiple layers to his story. His snoring indicated that he might have had sleep apnea, and as someone with sleep apnea myself, I know it can be a struggle if undiagnosed. Was he self-medicating with alcohol to help him sleep? Did he drink to cover the emotional pain that fueled his rage? I never saw him drunk, but I did feel his rage on several occasions. Thinking about it now, it seems that I never understood my dad until after he died.

# Secrets

Brown paper bags soaked in black
liquid, half-empty bottles stumbled
upon in the little house out back. The
strong odor slaps me senseless.

White shirt starched, a sharp crease in
your gray pants.
Your other side
is hidden from view.

# End of Summer

Why does it have to end? Green leaves
turn to gold, then to red, and on to
brown, before they fall and die.
Spring was not so long ago,
and summer cicadas still
cry out at dusk.
The full moon
whispers
of conversations and loved ones who
never really left.
The veil between the worlds
is very thin at this time of year.

Love life while you have it,
and enjoy the sun on your face
while it is still here,
before summer ends.

# Part Four:

*Adulthood*

(2000s, 2010s, and 2020s, ages fifty to seventy years old)

# Ten Sounds of Summer

1) When the cicadas come out at dusk, they sound like a whirring engine of an airplane that's about to take off.

2) The owls in the top field hoot from dusk to dawn. It is like they are texting each other, saying, "Hey, what's up?"

3) And then there are the peepers who live in the pond next door. They get excited and call out when it rains.

4) And then there is the cool summer rain. I hear its pinging sound on the chimney covers.

5) The fireworks popping on the Fourth of July is a childhood sound. I associate it with picnics and joy.

6) The laughter and clink of glasses filled with ice remind me of childhood fun, like eating vanilla ice cream on the front porch.

7) Then there is the sound of watermelon being split into bite-sized chunks on a paper plate. Clunk. Thud. Plop.

8) The sound of my black lab, Flip, as he plops down, panting, in the shade of his yard.

9) Old rock and roll tunes. "Sweet Home Alabama." "Carolina in My Mind."

10) James Taylor standing tall, playing guitar at the Virginia State Fair.

# Living in the Family Home

When my parents died, I inherited the family house. I was the only child, so I moved in and stayed because I am in love with the land. Living in my family home has been a spiritual and emotional experience for me.

People are often curious about what it is like to live in my childhood home. As with every place I've lived in my life, I thought I would only live there for a little while, but I ended up staying for several decades. The memories I have of the house are mixed. Some are happy, some are not so happy, and some are downright sad experiences that are difficult to talk about even now.

It's like the house is haunted by the past. Walking up the stairs to the second floor, I see myself as a little kid, sneaking downstairs in my footie pajamas on Christmas morning, then I hear my father screaming about the presents that have been left under the tree in the living room. Walking into what is now the dining room, I see my mother sleeping in her hospital bed.

On the upside, I feel protected by the spirit who lives on the land. My friend, Liz, who has a strong Shamanistic background, told me about this spirit when she visited me. She had a vision of the spirit, whom she said is named "Two Feathers," when she first visited me at the house. Two Feathers is a steward of the property. There are many arrowheads on the hillside, leftover from when Native Americans were the first inhabitants of the land. In my research of the area, I found that the property had a large Native American encampment in the woods before European settlers moved in and drove them away. I think of Two Feathers and ask for his help during big storms—real or imagined, I feel comforted by him. I often meditate and picture a white light of protection surrounding the house and all the oak trees during storms.

I have redone the whole house. I have painted, removed the carpet, taken down heavy curtains, and put framed paintings and photographs all over the house. The house is very warm. Friends comment on the "good vibes" when they come to visit. It is a lot like the warmth and love I had here as a very young child.

The ancient oak trees are a big asset to the property. Oak trees surround the house and cradle it in serenity. Whole families of oaks, evergreens, and magnolias live with me and surround me in their wisdom. I love to meditate on the flagstone in the front yard and soak in the oak tree energy. These trees are a great blessing in my life. They make me feel as though I live in an oak forest, like the Native Americans who camped here and rode their horses long before Europeans came to Virginia's shores. There is history here at my home, both good and bad—but then again, there is good and bad history to the whole Richmond area.

# Marriage Equality

In 2012, I stood in the voting area at the Baptist church I attended as a child and felt a clash of cultures. My Southern Baptist background screamed for me to vote for John McCain because he was a fine conservative white man. But the lines filled with laughing African American voters told me there was a new tide rising.

I have always identified with the outsider since I am also an outsider in many ways. I have always been the person who wanted to make a change, and now I had a chance to vote for change. Voting for hope and optimism and a man named Obama was intriguing. As a multiracial woman myself, I understood Obama. I, too, had many different racial ties pulling at me. There were complex currents inside him and inside me, and inside so many people at the time. I identified with him and felt a surge of electricity as I marked my vote for him.

That night, I stayed up very late to hear the election results on TV and cried when I saw Obama, Michelle, and their two young daughters cross the stage to accept his presidency. They looked so beautiful and confident. I also cried as I watched Obama and Michelle dance to "At Last," sung in person by Beyoncé, at the Inaugural Ball. At last, indeed.

But the moment that felt like lightning striking was when marriage equality became the law of the land in 2013. To have the president support LGBTQ rights was thrilling, to say the least. To see the rainbow flag projected on the outside of the White House in celebration of the event felt incredible. I still cry happy tears when I remember that scene on the six o'clock news. I am crying now as I write this memory.

On that day, I saw on Facebook that a local group was meeting for dinner in Carytown to celebrate. Part of me wanted to go out with them, but I knew there would be reporters and cameras (and I was right). I didn't think employers would like to see me on the six o'clock news, so I stayed home.

There is still much to be done for LGBTQ rights. Luckily, at the time I'm writing this, Joe Biden is president, and he has been a consistent ally for us. In fact, he was in favor of marriage equality even before Obama voiced his support. I remember Joe supporting us on *Meet the*

*Press*. It was an extraordinary and brave thing to do at the time. But there is still pushback from the far right, especially when it comes to trans rights. People on the far right feel very threatened by people who identify as transgender or nonbinary.

In Virginia, LGBTQ people and our allies are pushing back against this viewpoint. Recently, an eastern Virginia schoolboard and a trans high school student were in litigation over school bathrooms. The trans student wanted to use the bathroom that corresponded to his gender identity. The schoolboard said no. He won his case in the courts, though the school board has continued to appeal the case. This student has since happily gone on to college, and I wish him a happy life.

It is my hope that more and more of these cases have a happy ending like this one. It feels to me like we continue to take two steps forward and one step back in our progress as a nation. The fight must go on even if we get tired and feel discouraged. I really do think our founding fathers got it right when they wrote, "all men are created equal." Of course, I would like to add to the phrase "all women."

# Graduate School

One morning, I woke up early to get ready to go to work and knew in my heart that I needed to go to graduate school. I was still working as a counselor at a local college, though I had gone from part-time to full-time over the years. The voice in my head was loud and told me, in no uncertain terms, *If you want to teach, the time is now.* I was fifty years old—no longer a youngster—and I could hear the clock ticking. My intuition told me if I wanted to go back to school, the time was now. I still had energy and the desire to move ahead. I had always wanted to teach but feared I didn't have the time or money to go back to school. But I knew that I would never have the time or the money to go back, so I followed my intuition, and I jumped off the cliff feet first.

I applied to graduate school for reading education. I gathered my letters of recommendation and applied for student loans. I got in, and after a semester of both working full-time and attending school, it became obvious that I would need to make a choice: keep my current job or go back to school. I was terrified, but I chose to go back to school.

Taking out loans and commuting to the University of Virginia in Charlottesville over an hour away was hard. I connected with a church friend, Jeremy, who also commuted for his job there, and together, we were able to share the driving and the cost of gas. I owe him a debt of gratitude for his help with this commute.

In grad school, I was one of the oldest students in a young class. I was also one of the poorest, and I could feel the income inequality most of the time—I couldn't afford a nice laptop to do my homework on like the other students. Each afternoon, I waited in the library, doing my homework, for Jeremy to get out of work. I spent most of my time in tears. I was tired, frustrated, and overwhelmed.

It did not help that one of my professors was a perfectionist and proud of that fact. He joked that his coworkers said he had OCD. He thought they were joking, but honestly, I think they were trying to tell him something. We could not miss any classes, or he would automatically drop our grade one letter. One class missed; one letter grade dropped. Once, I had a bad cold but came to class, obviously sick. I was sneezing and coughing. My friends didn't want to get sick, so everyone sat several seats away from me in the front, back, and sides. The professor came by to see what the ruckus was and stood at the end of the aisle, looking at me as I sat, miserable, in my seat. Then he moved down the aisle. He made no comment.

# Teaching

After I graduated, I started as an adjunct reading instructor at the college where I had been a counselor. Each day, I hummed a happy tune on my thirty-minute drive to class. After picking up my mail from the division office, I walked upstairs to class, where I would engage students in talking about the readings and how their lives related to them. I loved it. They loved it. It was a lovefest for a very long time.

Then one day, I saw one of the full-time faculty, Martha Ann, carrying a basket full of pencils and chalk upstairs to teach, too. She asked me, "How many classes do you teach?" I told her one class and "I love it." She smiled wisely and said, "Good. That gives you a chance to enjoy them." Then she was off to her classes. What had she meant by that?

I went on to become a full-time instructor with five classes per semester, and twenty to thirty students per class, which of course meant twenty to thirty batches of papers per class, with endless revisions. I often picked unique subjects from the news for my students to write about because it gave them interesting things to say about their favorite subjects, which were usually abortion and marijuana legalization.

At the end of my teaching career, I was teaching on both campuses on a split schedule—morning classes on one campus and evening classes on the other. I would hold office hours between classes, and after dinner, I would walk Rayburn, the corgi I had adopted after the cocker spaniel, River, passed on, all before my evening thirty-minute commute to class. It turns out my evening students were just as tired as I was. They had been at work all day, usually in a restaurant, and would come to class after feeding their small children. They were often very motivated single moms who wanted more from life than waiting tables. I felt appreciated. They would tell me about their lives and how much I helped them.

I am retired now, but I miss my students and I miss teaching. My students were so motivated to change their lives and make a difference in their families, and I think I was so fond of them because I could identify with them. The odds had been against us, but we survived and thrived.

# One Thing I Learned

One thing I learned after I retired at age sixty-five is that those who say, "After you give up alcohol, life becomes the problem," are totally right. I wasn't an alcoholic, but I was a workaholic. I thought all the stress I felt when I was working was the problem. The backaches and trouble sleeping would disappear when I stopped working, or so I thought. I had been clenching my teeth so much that my doctor thought I must have heart problems, and I had to take stress tests. I even had to do an angiogram—that test where they pump dye through your veins and look at your heart for blockages. My health issues were so scary, but they were only symptoms of the real problem.

I found myself looking for personal connection at a time in life when it was hard to find it. It was as though I had been married to my job. People who aren't teachers don't understand it. "You have evenings and summers off," they tell you. "You have it good. Stop whining."

"Not really," was always my response. My evenings were spent answering emails and grading papers, even on Saturdays. During the summer, I only had a few weeks to rest before the next onslaught of work. For a few years, when I was chair of a program, I also used summers to do my program chair work, scheduling classes and hiring adjuncts and full-time instructors.

The void that was left by my retirement from full-time teaching was large. Now, I go for walks with my dog and volunteer at church with a small writing group. I always have several books I am reading by my nightstand. I belong to a second writers' group, paint landscapes in acrylic, and take photographs of my pets. But I am looking for another purpose. I want something to look forward to in my life, but not to consume it. Something that is a passion without being an addiction. And I have noticed that the hole of my childhood trauma, which overworking covered, has become much more obvious. There is much healing work to be done.

# Therapy

I first had therapy in my freshman year of college. The counselor at the University of Iowa told me she was glad I didn't have more serious mental health issues due to the way I grew up. This surprised me, but I was glad to hear my problems could have been worse. I have been in and out of therapy for most of the rest of my life, and each of my therapists has had a different philosophy and approach to my problems. Until recently, no one seemed to think I suffered from depression like my mother. But I have discovered that my childhood trauma affects nearly everything, from whom I love, to how I react to Christmas Day, when my father would scream over his disappointing presents.

One of my early therapists pronounced that my parents had "certainly lost it with me, but I certainly wasn't abused." This well-meant but incorrect pronouncement encouraged me to only work through things on the surface using affirmations and reframing. I meditated, which gave me some buffer between my sense of self and my sad personal story. I used a light box during rainy and cold times. I learned to respond rather than react. I agreed with Ruth King, my favorite meditation teacher, that life was neither "personal, permanent, nor perfect." I just wished I felt happier more of the time. Dan Harris, another mindfulness teacher and author, said that mindfulness had made him "ten percent happier," and he wrote a book by that title. I resigned myself to managing my expectations and taking life one day at a time.

Then I discovered eye movement desensitization and reprocessing, and a whole new world opened to me. EMDR is a form of therapy in which you visualize a triggering incident and reframe it in a way that tones down the intensity of the emotions. While visualizing the incident, you insert a positive affirmation; you can repeat the affirmation if the negative emotions reappear. For example, rather than focusing on what I can't do, I repeat, "I will be fine." Through this type of memory message reprogramming, I have been able to detach from childhood scripts that have been running my life from below the surface.

I learned through EMDR that I have often been attracted to charismatic but emotionally unavailable people who were like my dad. I also learned that I would hang on to an unworkable situation forever, trying to work it out, just like my parents did with each other. It sometimes takes me a while to recognize my patterns, but I do eventually see them. For example, I recently met a beautiful, charming woman from out of town who was emotionally unavailable, yet I was interested in dating her. She sounds a lot like my dad, doesn't she? It took me a while to get it, but I finally did.

# Stressful Dreams

I don't remember a time when I didn't have stressful dreams. When I was a child, I would wake up crying often enough that my mother slept in a spare bed in my room. For years, my dreams were about the black bear in the front yard. These dreams went away when I realized the bear was trying to tell me to listen and pay attention to my emotions so they wouldn't have to come roaring out from my subconscious in my dreams to get my attention. Both therapy and daily meditation have taught me to be in touch with my thoughts and emotions—to not push them away.

As an adult, my dreams are about getting lost. I can't figure out how to get off the interstate, or I can't figure my way out of a building. These dreams stopped when I figured out that they were a sign that I felt bogged down by making decisions. I have always been afraid of making a mistake.

Most recently, my stressful dreams have been about situations I need to face the next day. For example, I recently woke up processing things I need to say in EMDR about my grandmother's death. I wrote them down when I woke up and told my therapist about them.

At some point I want to learn to interact with the content of my dreams through lucid dreaming. I would like to have a discussion with myself about what to work on in therapy.

Dream self: "What would you like to do? Jump right in, right?"
Awake self: "God, no. Please pick something I can do easily."
Dream self: "But none of it is easy."
Awake self: "Oh yeah, you are right. Thanks."

I meditate every day, first thing in the morning. I have been doing this since 2001. My joke is that the Dalai Lama and I both sit on our beds every day after a shower to meditate. This is true—we just don't do it at the same time. I use a mantra that my Unitarian Universalist minister, Reverend Tom, taught me—a series of sounds that help me focus. For the last twenty years, I have gone to Unitarian churches because I appreciate how they combine truths from different spiritual paths. Humanism, science, Buddhism, Christianity, as well as New

Age beliefs can all be comfortably studied there. Reverend Tom is very embracing of all approaches to meditation, like good Unitarian Universalists tend to be. He also taught me about walking meditation too, as we walked outside our new church in the courtyard.

The type of meditation I practice now is very different from my brush with Transcendental Meditation in college. TM has strict rules to follow, so I left them behind. Strict rules have never been attractive to me since I escaped my Bible-quoting mother.

My thoughts about meditation are like the ongoing argument I had with my mother over how to do the dishes. According to her, there was a "right way and a wrong way" to do everything. I still feel there are many paths to get to the same place. There are many different routes to bypass the busy mind. I believe there are many paths to get to God—and heaven, too. Don't you agree?

# The Apology

I sat in the circle of twelve people in an awkward silence. It was my first visit to a medium at the Avalon Center, and it made me nervous. Patty, the medium, looked at her audience of varying ages wearing all kinds of clothes, from T-shirts to formal-looking clothes. My friend, Lucy, sat beside me. Lucy knew Patty and thought she was very good, which is why I had come. Patty, who was a heavyset woman, started to read the people seated on her right. She said she saw people inside their energy fields. I was on the left side of the room and closest to the door. Everyone listened to what Patty had to say, and most looked happy with her findings.

When Patty finally got to me, she told me I was a good person who had taken care of my parents for a long time. I asked her to see if I could talk with my grandmother, but Patty got a funny look on her face and told me someone else wanted to speak to me. He was a man who had pushed to the front of the line, saying he needed to talk to me.

"It must be my dad," I told her. No one else would be that pushy.

I sat in silence as he said three times that he was sorry. He said that most of my current problems were his fault, and he was sorry. He explained that he "was just trying to run the family like it was the army."

I was stunned. Clearly his life review had revealed a lot to him. I felt relieved for the first time in decades. My anger slipped away, revealing the wounded child underneath the surface. For the first time, I had a glimpse of what it would look like to heal all my childhood trauma. My anger began to slowly drain out of me, like a toxin.

At seventy, I am now the same age my parents were when I was in college. This is sobering for me because I always thought of my parents as old people. I don't think of myself as old, even though many people might describe me that way. When I look in the mirror, I see my mother's face and her wild curly hair. But the downturned lines around her mouth, which showed her habitual scowl, are not there on my face. Instead, I have deep crinkles around my eyes from smiling and laughing. I did not inherit my father's jet-black hair, but I did get his black eyes. I also inherited his love of painting and photography and my mother's love of dogs and cats. From my grandmother, I inherited a love of life and a love of Virginia's mountains.

But I also inherited the downside of the family gene pool. I have sleep apnea, which I think Dad and I shared. Nearly everyone on my mother's side of the family lived to be in their eighties, but my father's side died many years earlier than that. Diabetes runs in that side of the family, as it does in many Latino families. Luckily, I haven't had that problem, so far.

I am a southern, Latino Midwesterner. This blend gives me an eclectic approach to daily life that many of my friends find puzzling. For example, I can easily see myself having corn on the cob, grits with butter, and flan all in one meal. I am as at home in the mountains of Virginia as I am in the cornfields of Iowa or the beaches of Luquillo. I love the RVA arts scene as much as I loved seeing Patsy Cline play at the Chesterfield County Fair.

I recognize that my parents did their best for me. They loved me and wanted me to be happy. They also had their own demons to deal with. My childhood was the way it was due to critical parents and narrow choices in society. If my parents were alive today, we could go to counseling together and learn to talk about our feelings, be flexible, and make compromises together. These skills were absent in my childhood home and could have been learned. If I could talk to them now, I would tell my parents how much I loved them and that I still miss them.

# Where They Are Now

I have talked with Patricia every two weeks since the pandemic. We both appreciate the emotional touchstone that we have been for each other during this period of isolation. She has had the same home in the country and the same partner for more than a decade. I love both her and her mother, who I became close with when Patricia and I lived together. I call her mother on all the major holidays, and she still loves her history books, even though she is in her nineties. Patricia is happy in Iowa with her retired life. Like her mother, she loves history, and she's doing historical research now that she is retired.

Several years ago, I thought I had lost Patricia in a terrible accident. I got a phone message from her saying, "I am going on a helicopter on my way to the university hospital now. There has been an accident. I love you. Goodbye." It scared me to death. I could see her flying, semiconscious, over the Iowa landscape and landing on the roof of the university hospital, the highest building in the town. Thank God, she made it even though they had to put metal in her back and joints to hold her together. I don't know who I would have been if I hadn't known her.

During the pandemic, I reconnected with Dorothy. I talked with her once a month over Zoom during the pandemic. She has been living happily in the Northeast with her partner, Mona, for several decades. They live in a house full of fun travel memories.

Amanda lives in her family home in the countryside near Richmond. Her grandparents' farm has been sold, and she has a daughter who looks and sounds just like her.

I keep up with several friends I made while working in Iowa City. Karen and Terri volunteered with me at the crisis center. Terri is a social work instructor. Karen is a retired nurse. I lost touch with Kevin, who was my boss when I was there.

Marilyn still lives in Iowa, in a town south of Iowa City called Burlington, and she has several children and grandchildren whom she loves dearly.

Cindy and Sharon, my dorm friends, live in Texas. I keep in touch with Cindy.

Pam, my childhood buddy, lives in Florida.

# Gay in RVA

A lot has changed in Richmond since I was growing up in the fifties and sixties—thank God. There are places for LGBTQ people to meet, where there are people who understand and care for them, like Diversity Richmond, Richmond Lesbian Feminists, and Side by Side. People don't have to grow up feeling so alone anymore.

Sitting in my home office, watching a Zoom training to become a facilitator for an LGBTQ group, I am struck by how varied the meeting is. I am the oldest person in the room by thirty years, but I am happy I have finally stepped up to the plate. I had thought about this opportunity for a good twenty years, but worries about my age kept me back. I hope it will be a good experience for me, and for the group too.

I admit to being surprised by all the ways there are to identify now. I am happy for people coming out in this more open atmosphere. There are more choices and more freedom. I know that there are still obstacles. Hate groups are on the rise, and there's backlash to our progress. Kids are bullied, and some parents throw their children out of the house when they come out to them. But at least now there are backups.

Which brings me to why I am writing this book now. It seems to many young people that nothing ever really gets done. School shootings and global warming don't seem to be getting resolved. But if you look back at history, you can see that we really have come a long way. The police probably won't arrest you for dancing in a bar with your girlfriend, and if you want to get married to her, there are legal protections for you. Even though climate change is a pressing issue, most people realize that global warming is a serious problem and that if we want to have a beautiful planet, we need to take care of the earth and of ourselves.

In reading my story, I would like you to see my own resilience and strength as a metaphor for your own life. Our city and country have faced many challenges. The path forward has never been a straight one, but we have done our best. It has not always been easy for the LGBTQ community, but even as we face roadblocks and challenges, together we can prevail. We have prevailed before, and we can do it again.

It is my hope that Richmond will adopt a gay rights ordinance, protecting all its citizens. And I look forward to Carytown becoming a beacon of freedom. Someday soon, I hope to be able to walk down the street in Carytown, as I have seen others do, holding my partner's hand with comfort, safety, and love.

# About the Author

**M. J. Coll** is a retired English teacher and the author of book of poetry, *The Journey*. She has written essays for local Richmond magazines and newspapers about her experiences with anti-war protests, the second wave of feminism, and the beginnings of the current LGBTQ movement. She grew up in Richmond in the fifties and currently lives in the city with her black lab Flip.

www.ingramcontent.com/pod-product-compliance
Lightning Source LLC
LaVergne TN
LVHW011426080426
835512LV00005B/289